Vojislav Koštunica
and Serbia's Future

Norman Cigar

Vojislav Koštunica
and Serbia's Future

Foreword by
Sonja Biserko

Saqi Books
in association with
The Bosnian Institute

British Library Cataloguing-in-Publication Data
A catalogue record for this book is available from the
British Library

ISBN 0 86356 943 9 (pb)

copyright © 2001 Norman Cigar

This edition first published 2001

The Bosnian Institute
14/16 St Mark's Road
London W11 1RQ

Saqi Books
26 Westbourne Grove
London W2 5RH
www.saqibooks.com

Acknowledgements

The views in this study are entirely those of the author and do not necessarily reflect the policy or position of the United States government, the Department of Defense, or the Marine Corps. The author prepared this study while he was a Visiting Fellow at the Institute for Conflict Analysis and Resolution, George Mason University, Fairfax, Virginia, and wishes to express his gratitude to the faculty, fellows, and students for their collegiality and suggestions on this study, although the conclusions here are entirely those of the author. The study is based on information as of July 2001. The author also wishes to thank the Marine Corps University Foundation for its generous funding, which made possible travel for research to Bosnia-Herzegovina and to Kosovo.

Contents

Foreword

by
Sonja Biserko

Norman Cigar's study provides an accurate portrait of Vojislav Koštunica, one of contemporary Serbia's leading politicians and the successor to Slobodan Milošević as president of the 'Federal Republic of Yugoslavia' (FRY). Koštunica entered active politics as a young Law Faculty lecturer during the debate over the new – and in the event final – 1974 Constitution of the former Yugoslavia, which the Serbian military, political and intellectual establishment judged to be a challenge to Serbia's domination of the Yugoslav Federation. The promulgation of the 1974 Constitution, intended to secure after Tito's death the equality of the Federation's republics and provinces, set off a struggle for Tito's inheritance. The new Constitution was criticized in Serbia for allegedly fragmenting the 'Serb national body', while the republican and provincial borders were proclaimed to be 'a Communist invention': purely administrative and thus open to future change. This initial ideological basis for what was to culminate in Milošević's 'anti-bureaucratic revolution' of 1989 was supplied by a group of professors at the Belgrade University Law Faculty, together with the circle gathered around the former politician and writer Dobrica Ćosić; these became the main intellectual generators of Serb nationalism and promoters of the Serb national programme. Koštunica's strong support for the achievements of his predecessor as president of FRY is testified to by his recent (24 August 2001) statement that 'the cadres defeated at the 8th Session' – i.e. the 1987 meeting of the Serbian Central Committee at which Milošević came to power – 'are raising their heads again en masse, behaving as though the moment of their historical rehabilitation had arrived.'

Koštunica came to power in the same way as Slobodan Milošević: through a coup supported by conservative forces. He was presented to the public as an uncorrupted and honest politician, and a moderate nationalist committed to democracy and the rule of law. The West, increasingly frustrated in its relationship with Milošević, accepted this image of Koštunica readily and even enthusiastically, without scrutinizing his political and other activities during the ten years of crisis in the former Yugoslav area. Thanks to this frustration, and to the sense of guilt felt by some Western governments, FRY (or rather Serbia) was able to reintegrate within a few months into the international community, after fulfilling a minimum of conditions far less rigorous than those imposed on other post-Communist states of Eastern Europe. The international community gave up on Montenegro's independence, and postponed any resolution of Kosovo's status, on the grounds that these would destabilize the new 'democratic' Belgrade government. The surrender of Milošević to The Hague was used by both the ruling DOS coalition and the majority of Western states as additional evidence of a fundamental change for the better in Serbia, and in order to relativize the question of responsibility for a decade of war and war crimes.

It was only at the insistence of a number of NGOs that Western governments addressed such issues as the two thousand Albanian political prisoners held in Serbian jails, the continued links between the FRY and Republika Srpska (RS) armies, and FRY's cooperation with the Hague Tribunal. During the first few months, few of them paid attention to statements and moves on Koštunica's part showing unambiguously that his vision of Serbia conformed to the one held by Milošević; and that while Milošević and Koštunica differed at the ideological level, they shared the same territorial ambitions. Milošević's war efforts over a decade succeeded in encircling and ethnically cleansing 'Serb territories', leaving to Koštunica the task of achieving a 'spiritual and cultural unity of the Serb space'. Its political unification is for the time being postponed, due to unfavourable international circumstances. NATO's presence in Bosnia-Herzegovina, Kosovo and Macedonia forbids further military adventures. But the expansionist urge has remained. At the same time, there is a military agreement between Belgrade and Macedonia: according to General Pavković, the Serbian army is ready to 'help prevent a civil war in Macedonia'.

For a whole decade Koštunica's image on the Serbian political scene was that of 'Vojislav Šešelj in a frock coat', which explains why he commands today the support not just of Milošević's SPS, but also of Šešelj's Radical Party. Koštunica was deeply involved in the events in RS, which along with northern Kosovo remains one of his main strongholds. He himself has stated that in its programme and policy his party, DSS, is closest to Radovan Karadžić's SDS. The Serb Orthodox Church, one of the bastions of Milošević's and Karadžić's drive for the creation of a Greater Serbia, is likewise a main supporter of Koštunica's policy, whose contours became evident with symbolic visits at the start of his presidency: to Trebinje in RS for the reburial of nationalist poet Jovan Dučić, to Hilander monastery on Mount Athos, and to Russia where characteristically he had a private audience with Patriarch Alexei III before meeting President Putin. The West, meanwhile, serves as a source of financial aid.

Koštunica's attitude to the Hague Tribunal as an object of contempt remains unchanged today. He has publicly attacked Milošević's arrest and extradition and has done what he could to present himself as someone who believes that the Tribunal is anti-Serb. He agreed to the delivery of Milošević for financial reasons, but continues to foster 'Serb dignity' and an anti-Western stance. FRY will cooperate with The Hague, but 'with full national and state dignity'. By conviction he espouses a Pan-Orthodox world view that is rooted in irrevocably anti-Western sentiment and, therefore, remains a permanent source of instability in the Balkans. His power continues to be based on the Army, the Church, Milošević's former establishment, and the circle around

Dobrica Ćosić. The recent assassination of former security-service agent Gavrilović has thrown new light on his role in protecting the old structures, including people who could be indicted by the Hague Tribunal. He has amnestied the Army, which is the main bastion of his support, from all responsibility for war crimes, arguing that it 'has always behaved in accordance with the law, including its highest officers'.

Cigar's presentation of Vojislav Koštunica's personality comes at the right moment, when the West is still undecided in regard to the region and its main actors. During the past ten months Koštunica has displayed his true nature and the West has started increasingly to condition its support, especially of a financial nature. The decade-long Balkan crisis has now entered a new phase with the outbreak of conflict in Macedonia. This new crisis, however, cannot be seen in isolation from FRY and Kosovo. Belgrade has always linked the future of Kosovo to that of Macedonia, placing both in the context of a general re-composition of the Balkans. In 1992 a warning by US President George Bush against Belgrade's interference in Macedonia was followed by a UN mission. Today the Macedonian issue has been reactivated and Koštunica, believing this is the end game, is relying on Russia and Orthodoxy. But this insistence on a political re-composition of the Balkans is distracting Serbia and its citizens from embarking on the necessary process of transition. Serbia is a devastated land, which for a long time now has been displaying signs of xenophobia, introversion and intolerance. The diversion of social energy to an essentially defeated political project threatens further social radicalization. Serb nationalism caused Yugoslavia's break-up and now it imperils Serbia too. This is why it is important for the international community to re-evaluate its strategy towards Serbia and, by confronting Vojislav Koštunica's role and political vision, to gain a better grasp of the country's internal situation. This book will prove invaluable for this purpose.

Sonja Biserko is president of the Helsinki Committee for Human Rights in Serbia, and editor of its monthly journal Helsinška povelja. *She is currently on a visiting research fellowship at the United States Institute for Peace in Washington DC*

Introduction

The Federal Republic of Yugoslavia (FRY), established in April 1992 by Serbia and Montenegro, remains a country burdened by active or latent conflicts, both internally and with a number of its neighbors. The political views of its new president, Vojislav Koštunica, are not the only ones represented in the coalition that has governed the country since October 2000; nevertheless, the nature of his leadership will have a great influence on how, or whether, those conflicts are resolved, with potential consequences for both FRY itself and the region as a whole. President Koštunica, who heads one of the parties in the new coalition government – the Democratic Party of Serbia (Demokratska stranka Srbije [DSS]) – has often been portrayed in the West as the inspirer of a new beginning, and as the moving force for the democratization of FRY (and in particular of Serbia, where his party plays a key role), after the removal of the authoritarian system which Slobodan Milošević ran for some thirteen years.[1] Indeed, *Time* magazine honored Koštunica as a runner-up to President George W. Bush as 'Person of the Year' for 2000, while the New York-based East West Institute honored him in May 2001 as 'Statesman of the Year' in a ceremony attended by an array of international celebrities.

This study examines President Koštunica's actual and potential role, both in conflict and in conflict resolution, by looking at the interpretative framework or mental model – here called a 'paradigm' – that has been basic to his outlook. The inquiry is not just a theoretical one: only if we understand the basic framework of Koštunica's mental world shall we be able to gauge his likely policy choices, and the impact he may have in dealing with present and future conflicts. The main finding of this study is that although President Koštunica represents a break in some ways with Milošević, his interpretative model and his policy goals have been, and remain, those of Greater Serbian nationalism. If these remain unchanged, they are likely to have little more success in producing genuine conflict resolution (a durable agreement achieved through a collaborative process), or even conflict settlement or conflict management at a lower level, than did those of his predecessor. Indeed, he could potentially make some conflicts even worse.[2]

In many cases the active or potential conflicts involving Serbia (in relation to Kosovo, the Sandžak, Croatia, Bosnia, the Roma community, or the ethnic Bulgarian areas) have an ethnic aspect to them. In some other cases, such as those of Montenegro or Vojvodina, contention has centered primarily on political and constitutional issues – although here too there is at least a partial overlap with an ethnic issue. In all these cases, however, conflict ultimately revolves around the basic concept of the Serbian state and community, and the desirability of a nationalist ideological framework. Some of the issues just mentioned are not cases of the intractable type of conflict with which the discipline of conflict resolution is particularly concerned; but the possibility of development into that type of conflict cannot be excluded, even in those cases. Unless resolved in time, even peaceful conflicts could become violent. Indeed, in the case of Montenegro there is the precedent of World War II, which saw one of the most vicious internecine conflicts occur on its soil, even though ethnicity did not play a significant role there.

It is true that Koštunica has been in office for only a comparatively short time, which means that any assessment of his performance so far might qualify only as a 'snapshot' in a developing situation. Nevertheless, we already have some indications – concrete policy initiatives, as well as declaratory statements – of his concept of statecraft in relation to conflicts. And in many ways the initial orientation of his administration during this formative period may indicate the direction it will take, and may determine the character of his approach in the longer term. At the time of writing, the future of FRY itself remains unsure, because of the evolving status of Montenegro within the federation. If Montenegro were to opt for independence at some time in the future, this would leave a 'Yugoslavia' consisting only of Serbia; as an alternative, one could expect at the very least a redrawing of the political relationship between the two partners within the federal framework. But Koštunica is likely to remain a major factor on the political scene for the foreseeable future, whether at the helm of FRY or at that of Serbia – the presidency of which has continued to be occupied by a place-holder left over from the Milošević era (and an indicted war criminal, to boot).

Whatever Koštunica's personal political future may be, the aim of this study is also to provide insights into the prospects for conflict resolution in Serbia over a longer time-frame, and more broadly to illustrate the importance of mental models or 'paradigms' in dealing with conflict in any society.

Terms of Reference

Paradigms and the analysis of conflict

Thomas S. Kuhn's pioneering work on the significance of 'paradigms' in the history of the natural sciences had implications for the social sciences as well, including conflict resolution studies.[3] In a seminal work, Robert Jervis applied this concept to decision-making in international relations, looking at the ways in which paradigms operate in human interactions.[4] How leaders analyse a conflict, and what elements or methods they see as relevant to its solution, may depend upon the paradigms they hold – what Sandole calls 'collective internalized maps'. These mental models or maps can thus play a major role in how the conflict is perceived, and whether it is addressed and resolved.[5] Out of a welter of facts, some data have to be selected as relevant: as Kuhn noted with regard to the natural sciences, some paradigm will invariably be present to make this possible. Otherwise, 'In the absence of a paradigm or some candidate for a paradigm, all the facts that could possibly pertain to the development of a given science are likely to seem equally relevant.'[6] Policy-makers too have to formulate paradigms or models, whether consciously or unconsciously, in order to make sense of problems and to organize and interpret the information they need for decision-making – though, of course, the relation between the paradigm and the decision is neither mechanistic nor necessarily uniform. As Richard K. Betts has put it: 'Preconceptions cannot be abolished; ["preconception"] is in one sense just another word for "model" or "paradigm" – a construct used to simplify reality, which any thinker needs in order to cope with complexity.'[7]

Once established, such mental models are likely to have a significant impact on policy-making; they may also (as in this case) affect the chances of conflict resolution. Paradigms based on misperceptions, or on questionable assumptions, or on faulty or incomplete information, can result in flawed and counter-productive policies. Eliminating the sources of a conflict can hardly be achieved if the nature of the underlying problem is not correctly identified.[8] And if the problem is misrepresented, the policies chosen to deal with it will probably end in failure.[9]

Level of analysis

The level of analysis in this case is President Koštunica as an individual. While Sandole has shown that a full analysis of a conflict must be a complex thing, dealing with contributory factors at many levels, it is nevertheless true that focusing on one key element can cast light on the larger problem.[10] One does not have to subscribe to the 'great man' theory of history to appreciate the impact that an individual leader can have on a society, and on the policy choices that are made or even considered. This is particularly true of a society such as Serbia's, with its tradition of patriarchal politics.[11] Of all the major Serbian parties, it is perhaps the DSS that has had the weakest organizational structure and has relied most on the personality of its leader to attract votes.

In many ways, Vojislav Koštunica's education and family background have shaped his views and political activity to this day. He was born in Belgrade in 1944 in a staunchly anti-Communist family, but maintains ties to his family village of Koštunici, some three hours from Belgrade, and thus has roots in Serbia's heartland (although his family does originate from Herzegovina in earlier generations). As a native Serb, he has had a built-in advantage over potential rivals born outside Serbia, such as Zoran Đinđić, Vuk Drašković, or Vojislav Šešelj, and even

Slobodan Milošević with his Montenegrin roots, who have invariably been seen as *prečani*, or outsiders.[12]

Koštunica earned a B.A. from Belgrade University's Law School in 1966, an M.A. in 1970, and his doctorate in law in 1974. His training in constitutional law, in particular, in many ways has marked his approach to conflict analysis and resolution throughout his career, with a penchant for legalistic arguments. In 1974, he was dismissed from his job at the university for opposing the introduction of the new Constitution under then-President Tito, which decentralized the Yugoslav state and granted greater autonomy to Kosovo and Vojvodina.[13] As an academic Koštunica thereafter worked at the Institute for Social Sciences and at the Institute for Philosophy and Social Theory, and has written widely in the fields of constitutional law and political theory, as well as serving as editor for a number of academic journals. He notably co-authored with Kosta Čavoški *Stranački pluralizam ili monizam* [Party pluralism or monism] (1983), the first attempt in Communist Yugoslavia to rehabilitate the pre-war Serbian political parties.

With the systemic changes of the late 1980s and the more liberal environment, however, Koštunica became increasingly involved in politics. He was one of the founders, with Zoran Đinđić and others, of the Democratic Party (Demokratska stranka – DS) in 1989, and was elected to Serbia's Parliament in 1990, where he served until 1997. However, internal divisions within DS over the issue of whether or not to cooperate with the Milošević government – 'significant programmatic and tactical differences', as they are described today – soon fostered the development of two rival wings. Despite the fact that many of the opposition parties, including the DS, had formed a broader coalition (DEPOS) in the spring of 1992, internal differences within the DS were to lead to the creation and breaking away of the Democratic Party of Serbia (Demokratska stranka Srbije – DSS) on 26 July 1992, under the leadership of Koštunica, which held its first congress in December 1992. The break-up of the DS is instructive not only in terms of Koštunica's personal world-view, but also helps explain his enduring hostile relationship with Đinđić, as his principal rival within the original DS, and helps to understand the policies which Koštunica and the

DSS have pursued ever since. The break-up appears to have been unusually acrimonious, with the DS retaining all party assets, which obliged the newly-established DSS to operate for a while from the Astoria Hotel.

The addition of 'Serbia' to the name of the new party was in itself indicative of Koštunica's outlook. As he noted at the time, the stress on Serbia 'is not accidental' and was meant to convey the idea that Serbia was the focus; but at the same time he stressed that there were implications beyond Serbia's borders. As he remarked, the intended process of political change (or 'democratization' as he termed it) within Serbia could 'lead the Serbs outside of Serbia into another type of relationship [i.e. with Serbia], and to the political and cultural unity of the Serbs throughout the area of the former Yugoslavia, which is one of the basic goals of the DSS.' Specifically, this process, which Koštunica said might occur 'in phases', would be possible if Serbia itself developed into a 'strong and democratic state'.[14] To a great degree, disagreement with the DS had hinged on what the DSS saw as the DS's unbalanced focus on democracy and economic development to the detriment of attention to the national question. In retrospect, as the DSS's official website still stresses, the deciding issue at the time had been that, in contrast to its rivals within the DS, the future members of the DSS believed that: 'The Serb question within Yugoslavia was neither a question of political democracy nor of economic equality, but rather a question of the national survival of the Serb nation.' Indeed, 'the other wing of the Democratic Party deluded itself that it was possible to reach short-term understandings with the [Milošević] regime, and that the regime could be democratized from within. For [this wing], the national question practically either did not exist or it hinged on the thesis of the special responsibility of the Serb nation, as the largest [nation], for the preservation of Yugoslavia.' Citing irreconcilable differences over the national issue, the DSS withdrew from the DEPOS coalition in mid-1993. The DSS also held aloof from the Zajedno coalition which battled Milošević during the winter of 1996–97, again arguing that the national issue was being ignored by the coalition.[15] By 2000, however, apparently concluding that a go-it-alone stand would favor the continuation of Milošević in power, the DSS decided to participate in the broad-based Democratic Opposition of Serbia (DOS), with Koštunica as candidate for President of FRY, setting the stage for Milošević's ultimate defeat in the September 2000 election.

Although the focus here may be on an individual, the paradigm and the beliefs held by that one person are not just private things: they are shared by a significant number of like-minded people in his society, particularly within the political class. This study is concerned with Koštunica's public role in the political realm. It does not try to examine the inner motivations for his personal belief system – even though a deeper analysis of the psychological and biographical origins of that system of beliefs might shed further light on its strength and durability.

Constructing Koštunica's ideological résumé: forming a paradigm during the opposition years

In order to understand the mental framework of President Koštunica's decision-making today, this study looks at his ideological and intellectual development in the years before he came to power in October 2000. It then examines his recent statements and policy initiatives (however limited so far), and correlates them with his earlier world-view, to see what degree of change or continuity there has been. This makes it possible to gauge the prospects for conflict resolution. Views that remain consistent over time can be regarded as embedded ideological and intellectual patterns: these tell us what analytical filters are fixed in his mind, and can serve as a guide to his future actions. To be sure, a politician may change as he takes up new responsibilities, and he may moderate earlier paradigms, or completely discard them, in response to the constraints of the situation, negative feedback, or failure in the real world. In some historical cases, political figures have indeed 'grown' in their new roles; in other cases, however, their policies have continued to reflect the dominance of their enduring systems of belief, and have merely become a concrete expression of their earlier views.

To a great extent, one overriding paradigm has provided the basic framework of Koštunica's goals and policies for at least the past decade. His vision of Serbia and the Serbs requires particular attention: this is what lies behind his attitude to most conflicts involving Serbia, to Serbia's relations with the international community, and even to the domestic political environment. Drawing on Koštunica's writings and on the interviews he gave during his many years in political opposition, this study aims to identify the key elements of his ideological and intellectual framework, and to show how that framework has been applied to cases of actual or latent conflict since his coming to power in October 2000.

A Nationalist Paradigm

A Vision of Serbia and the Serbs

For Koštunica, his core paradigm over the years has been one related to his vision for Serbia. Specifically, what has driven other considerations has been what is usually called a traditional nationalist concept of 'Greater Serbia': that is, the goal of including as many Serbs living throughout the former Yugoslavia into a single Serb state as possible. As Serbia developed its statehood in the 19th century, it initiated an expansion of its borders over the next two centuries, while a vision of the ultimate extent of the state became the guiding principle for policy and legitimacy. Usually, this has come to be identified as the goal of a 'Greater Serbia': that is, the intent to encompass into a single state all lands claimed to be 'Serbian', even when, as has often been the case, Serbs constituted only a minority of the population in a given area. As a corollary, policies of subordination or removal through ethnic cleansing of non-Serbs often accompanied the acquisition of new territories.[16] However, the implementation of this ideology has had both long-term and recent historical baggage for non-Serbs, who have seen it as an aggressive objective to be implemented at their expense. Clearly, there could be no way to fulfill this agenda without using force to absorb or carve up neighboring republics and to eliminate the non-Serb population which has constituted the majority in many of the areas earmarked for expansion. As such, adherence to this goal was, and has remained, a non-negotiable and inherently destabilizing starting-point for inter-communal relations and central to most of the conflicts in the former Yugoslavia involving Serbia. Yet it was precisely this goal which served as the guiding principle for Koštunica during his years in opposition, shaping his assessment of and response to most policy issues. What Koštunica defined as the overriding problem while he was in opposition was that, as he saw it, the Serbs had been oppressed in the former Yugoslavia in terms of having their nationalism suppressed. According to Koštunica, only the Serbs had been good Yugoslavs, and he claimed that: 'While some built during the day, others destroyed at night . . . Today, we know who were the builders and who were [Yugoslavia's] destroyers.' The Serbs, moreover, had been forced to accept what he viewed as the former Yugoslavia's unfair republic borders ('Those borders were practically imposed'), and he claimed that the Serbs alone of all the ethnic communities were thus left divided.[17] In his view, even the setting up of Vojvodina as an autonomous province within Serbia in 1945 (rather than making it an integral part of the latter) was suspect, since he claimed it had been done only for 'historical, cultural, and traditional' reasons, even though the Serbs there had been in the majority.[18]

Basically, according to Koštunica, the Serbs were the only nation denied its national rights: 'Since all the nations of the former Yugoslavia put forward their national demands, is only the raising of the Serb question before and after the fall of Yugoslavia controversial?'[19] After Yugoslavia's disintegration, the threat was portrayed as one to the Serbs both in terms of a state and of their very identity and this provided the basis for Koštunica's political activity. When asked what his basic beliefs were, he replied: 'When I speak of my credo, I think of two things: on the one hand of the commitment that our national being (*korpus*) be preserved, whether it is a case of our national territories or our national values. My personal and party activity in that respect is conservative, since it does not seek to conquer but only to preserve values.' Because of what he viewed as a non-nationalist Milošević government, Koštunica continued, the identity of the Serbs was most threatened in Serbia itself: 'It is here that the need is clearest for national consciousness to be awakened, in the state in which the majority of the people are Serbs. Without the Serbs, this state [i.e. Yugoslavia] would not even have been created, and yet it does not even carry the Serbian name . . . in the home country [i.e. Serbia], at the center of Serbdom, the situation is worse than it has ever been before. That is where my extra motivation for political involvement comes from.'[20]

Koštunica's solution to what he saw as the overriding problem of the Serbs' deprivation of national rights and identity was a rejection of the Yugoslav concept, which had competed with that of a Greater Serbia in the 19th and 20th centuries. On the contrary, he opted for 'the gradual resolution of its [i.e. Serbia's] state issue, step by step and in a radically different manner than the attempt to solve this issue in 1918 and later [i.e. Yugoslavia]. More precisely, that means establishing a Serbian national state among the [other] states of this region which are also national ones. That is a simple answer, though the paths and mechanisms to achieve that are more complicated and require more time . . .'[21] As he saw it, Serbia and Montenegro would 'gradually become a magnet to gather the Serbian territories.'[22] He openly stressed the need for Serbia to expand: 'Only with the continued survival of the Republika Srpska will Serbia continue to have two lungs. Without the western lands [i.e. territories in Bosnia-Herzegovina], Serbia would become an invalid, with only a single lung.'[23] And, as he had added, 'A consciousness must exist that on both sides of the Drina [i.e. in Bosnia too] lives a single people which, naturally, strives to create a single state.'[24]

This goal of a single, expanded, Serbian state was enshrined in the official platform of the DSS which Koštunica headed, namely in the call to create a 'state which would extend over the entire Serb ethnic space, when the current, extremely unfavorable, international conditions change'; and this was, in fact, equated to the 'Serbian national interest.'[25] As one of the DSS's vice-presidents emphasized, 'Our basic position on the national issue is well-known . . . the right to that which represents our basic goal, that is a single Serb state . . . There are no changes in that.'[26]

In addition, what was needed was a revived nationalist outlook, and to that end the DSS platform stressed that: 'The DSS believes that it is above all important to effect a spiritual renewal of the

Serbian nation in order to eliminate the spiritual void and national indifference which are the consequence of the many years of Communist rule and of the illusion of Yugoslavism.'[27]

However, according to Koštunica, after Yugoslavia's disintegration the Serbs were being forced to live in three separate 'unrecognized and disputed' states (Serbia, and the parastates of Republika Srpska and the RSK carved out in Bosnia and Croatia respectively), while what he scornfully viewed as artificial non-Serb nations – that is, the Bosniaks and Macedonians – had their own countries: 'Those nations born, or more exactly created, in Communist Yugoslavia, which thanks to the Communist government achieved consciousness of a national identity and began to see and began to walk in national terms, got their hands on their own states.'[28] And he complained that legitimate Serb nationalism was being blocked by countries which he felt had engaged in similar nationalist practices, claiming that it was American patriotism which had allowed for expansion to Vietnam, Soviet patriotism to Afghanistan, British patriotism to the Malvinas (Falklands), and French patriotism to New Caledonia, 'but Serbian [patriotism] only to the Drina [river] and not one step farther.'[29] In fact, Koštunica portrayed the threat to the Serbs as extreme, with the very existence of the nation at stake: 'The basic nationalist goal is above all survival, that is the salvation of this nation.'[30]

As a corollary, traditional Serbian nationalism has also championed Serbia as an exclusivist national state, at times resulting in the actual or planned elimination of non-Serb communities. Koštunica, here too, would hew true to the traditional view, as he promoted the concept of a national Serb state in which the Serbs would be dominant, and opposed what he saw as the Milošević government's concept of Serbia (whether or not Milošević was sincere in that respect) as 'a multi-national community or a miniature Yugoslavia'. Koštunica criticized such notions, including Serbia's 1990 Constitution in which, he said, Serbia 'was defined as the state of all the citizens of Serbia.' He disagreed with such a view, countering that: 'Such claims do not correspond to the true state of affairs. A national minority, as is the case of the Albanians for us, cannot attain a special status. Thus, for us, the ethnic structure in Serbia is the same as it is in any state in the West, in which alongside the dominant nation there are also representatives of other nations and that does not change the fact that those are national states.' For him, all non-Serbs could be only minorities within a national Serb state: 'Serbia should be the state of the Serbian people; and, of course, the state of all who live there, with the appropriate rights.'[31]

Koštunica was also critical of the democratic opposition, whom he accused of promoting a civil, as opposed to a national, state for Serbia. As he said, he was clearly unhappy that: 'Serbia is not felt to be the state of the Serbian people, but rather – again – a multinational state. That is the position of the ruling regime, but also of individual loud spokesmen of the opposition.'[32] As Koštunica concluded, 'It would be preferable according to our party's positions if Serbia were the state of the Serbian people and, of course, also the state of all those who live there, along with rights appropriate to them.'[33] Apparently sensitive to the fact that such nationalist goals might elicit criticism, Koštunica sought to convince audiences that: 'This is pleading not for a Greater Serbia, but for a normal democratic Serbian state' – although in practice it would be difficult to make such a differentiation on the basis of his stated goals.[34]   To be sure, Koštunica has always insisted that he is both a democrat and a nationalist. But in this context one has to appreciate how Koštunica himself understands 'democracy' and the balance between that and nationalism, since this may have a major impact on how he approaches conflicts. As he saw it, democracy does not mean a civil society: 'We seek to harmonize a democratic and nationalist policy, while the "civil"-imbued circles believe that people can be exclusively citizens and nothing else, without a nationalist consciousness, without religious feelings, and without a past.'[35] Indeed, he lambasted those in favor of a 'civil option' for being 'uncritical and idolatrous' toward the international community, which he claimed 'can only prolong Serbia's ghettoization in a different manner, placing Serbia in a semi-colonial status, as is the case with some other former Communist countries.'[36] Lumping together the Milošević government and 'part of the opposition cosmopolitans in Serbia' for their alleged failure to promote Serbian nationalism, he accused them all of accepting the fait accompli, 'almost enthusiastically.'[37]

However, the concept of a nationalist state has been problematic for Serbia. Not only have Serbs become only a slight – and rapidly declining – majority within Serbia itself (if one includes Vojvodina and Kosovo), but the dilemma would have become even more pronounced in the event of an expansion into neighboring republics such as prominent Serb nationalist figures were advocating by the late 1980s.[38] What is more, the growth rate of the Serbs is negative, whereas that of some of Serbia's minorities (Albanians, Roma, Bosniaks) is very high, indicating that within a generation the Serbs themselves will become a minority, further complicating the notion of a 'national' state.

Paradoxically, for Koštunica, any problem surrounding Kosovo and Vojvodina (as former autonomous provinces within Serbia and de facto republics on their own since 1974) had been 'solved' in 1989, with Milošević's suppression of their autonomy, and would remain so throughout most of this early period. Koštunica appears to have had an abiding aversion for the autonomy which the 1974 Constitution granted to Vojvodina and Kosovo, and for the reduced central control from Belgrade over the country's other republics that it enshrined. According to an interview with his wife, in fact, he had been ousted as a junior faculty member from the law school of the University of Belgrade specifically for protesting the introduction of the 1974 Constitution.[39]

Even as many in the Serb political elite abandoned or tempered their earlier calls for a Greater Serbia as unfeasible in the wake of opposition by the international community, military defeats at the hands of non-Serbs, and a tepid popular response within the Serb community to long-term war, Koštunica continued to see this as a benchmark for patriotism. What is more, he attacked bitterly both the Milošević government and what he termed 'the so-called opposition in Serbia' for what he disparagingly called their limited perspective, which he claimed: 'is based on the old, never corroborated myth that Serbia across the Drina [i.e. in Bosnia] is up for dispute, [that it is] Greater Serbia, while Serbia up to the Drina, if possible reduced in the North [i.e. Vojvodina] and South [i.e. Kosovo] in its head and legs, is the true, allowable, Serbia. Of course, ever since Yugoslavia has been in existence, Serbia has been a single indivisible space on both sides of the Drina, and the Serbs here and over there [i.e. in Bosnia] are a single and the same people. Notwithstanding what foreigners and domestic peaceniks (*miroljupci*) have thought and said, peace can be established more quickly by accepting this natural fact than by rejecting it.'[40]

When the opposition to Milošević coalesced in the winter of 1996–97, Koštunica was asked whether the DSS's support for the Bosnian Serbs would change. He reassured his audience that: 'I have said that nothing will change . . . My visit to Pale [i.e. Karadžić's headquarters] and talks with the leadership of Republika Srpska at the time that the "Zajedno" [opposition] coalition began to function, and then the statements I made at the rallies in Serbia, best illustrate that our national policy and our stand on Republika Srpska will not change.'[41]

Ends, ways, and means

Establishing a single Serb national state ('solving' the problem as he defined it) not only remained elusive but also, not unexpectedly, raised the dilemma of whether it was possible to do so without using systematic and large-scale violence. Significantly, Koštunica was a strong supporter of the Bosnian Serb leadership and the latter's war effort, and was critical of Milošević's draw-down of aid to the latter as a means of exerting pressure. Indeed, Koštunica accused Milošević of having let down the Bosnian Serbs as they fought their war, openly terming such policy 'national betrayal toward the Serbs across the Drina'.[42] In the dispute which pitted the Bosnian Serb leadership and Milošević over the wisdom of continuing the war and holding out for maximum objectives, Koštunica came out squarely in favor of Karadžić and his coterie. According to his assessment, the latter represented good nationalists or, as he termed it, 'a healthy nationalist substance. That [part of] our nation can help strengthen the feeling of belonging to Serbdom [*srpstvo*], which has become significantly weakened in the large cities in the homeland [i.e. in Serbia].'[43] However, as the difficulty of achieving such goals militarily became evident over time, Koštunica began to stress that an expanded Serb national state could be achieved by other means, such as by the use of diplomacy: 'we believe that through negotiations we can gradually create the contours of such a state. Of course, we do not think like the SPS that the national question can be resolved piece-meal, up to the Drina and [separately] beyond the Drina.'[44]

Koštunica saw the international community, and particularly the United States, as threatening and a major obstacle to the achievement of Serb nationalist goals. He has felt that it was the United States which had the final say, concluding that when the European Union had favored suspending the sanctions against FRY, their decision 'fell before just a single American "No".'[45] In fact, he viewed French President Charles de Gaulle as a role model, for having been conscious of the 'danger from American hegemony.'[46] However, Koštunica continued to hold out hope that his enduring goals might become feasible with time even if not attainable at present because, as he saw it, of the US's hostile dominance: 'American hegemony rules in the world . . . [but] there are democrats in the world who criticize this order; this order is not eternal, just as no other international order is eternal.'[47]

Even after coming to power, Koštunica continued to hold such views: 'And when I refer to "imposed peace", I do not have in mind only Kosovo. I refer to what is called the "pax Americana", all sorts of American peace treaties which in many cases endeavor to solve problems in a way that does not suit the reality of those countries.'[48] Nevertheless, he was hopeful that 'the changes in personalities' with a new US Administration would 'make all of that easier' and result in a policy change.[49]

Koštunica also blamed Milošević's 'manipulation' for supposedly having helped a misunderstanding of Serb policy to emerge abroad, specifically 'what is attributed to the Serbs, that is, nationalism. That nationalism does not exist.'[50] At times, Koštunica was also critical of Milošević for allegedly being too accommodating to the international community. After the fall of the 'Krajina' in 1995, Koštunica railed that: 'Every concession by it [i.e. the government in Belgrade] leads to new and more extensive demands by the international community. The list of demands continuously grows longer.[51] Eventually, however, a hallmark of Koštunica's public discourse became his criticism of Milošević for – on the contrary – confronting the international community and dragging the Serbs into unsuccessful wars. For example, he blamed Milošević for 'the responsibility for the reckless warmongering policy of 1990 and 1991, which was avoidable,' and for 'the ruinous war which he initiated in 1991.'[52] Again, he viewed Serb soldiers and policemen as having 'died needlessly' in the Kosovo War.[53]

However, Koštunica repeatedly argued that it was the methods used, rather than the goals themselves, which were problematic: 'The real question at this moment is: is the goal which we support legitimate? That [goal] is the right to self-determination and to one's own state. I reply that this goal is legitimate, [but] that it could not be achieved by the means which this regime has used. There are other means which show that support for this is far from being liable to be characterized as warlike. That is, we want long-term peace.'[54]

At the same time, one cannot conclude that Koštunica's analytical outlook was directed against violence per se in support of nationalist goals or that he excluded this as a way to resolve conflicts. On the contrary, one can argue that, at least in part, Koštunica's criticism of a war option was linked to his appreciation of the balance of power, which he came to see as largely stacked against Serbia. Confronting the reality of a weak Russia, Koštunica assessed that: 'As a small nation, we must act according to the balance of power in the world. The world as we knew it earlier no longer exists. There is no longer any balance. Today, we have a unipolar world in which the power of only one country, the USA, is exceptional and the former great USSR empire, or the Russia which has remained from that, has great internal problems.'[55] However, Koštunica urged that potential rifts between Europe and the US be exploited.[56]

This nationalist frame of reference might also help account for Koštunica's penchant to ignore or at best minimize war crimes committed by Serb perpetrators. Acceptance that war crimes, much less genocide, had occurred at all – and the implication that this may not have been an isolated phenomenon, but inherent in the Serb nationalist agenda – would be difficult to reconcile with his more noble articulations of a Greater Serbia. In this respect, Koštunica has been reluctant to acknowledge war crimes committed by the Serb side, ostensibly because the evidence is lacking, but probably more realistically because that would tarnish the legitimacy of pursuing long-cherished goals and clash with his idealistic view of Serb nationalism. To be sure, in the course of events Serbs too have often been victims; but Koštunica has sought to direct the focus almost entirely to that phenomenon, while ignoring, minimizing, or rejecting the cases of the many more numerous victims of Serbian policy. A failure to recognize, much less investigate and prosecute, war crimes is likely only to complicate meaningful attempts at conflict resolution with non-Serbs.

Typically, he offered the standard disclaimer about Serbia's military involvement beyond its borders, asserting that Serbia was not involved in Bosnia and complaining that the international community 'placed sanctions on those not fighting,' that is on Serbia – ignoring the fact that it was common knowledge that the Serb war effort in neighboring countries was decisively supported, and in many respects managed, from Belgrade.[57] Likewise, in the case of Sarajevo, he opined at the time that there was no difference between the defenders and the attackers: 'On one side the Serbs hold Sarajevo in their [gun] sights, while Izetbegović's troops hold [Sarajevo] in their sights from inside.'[58] Asked about an earlier statement that Srebrenica had been 'a defensive action by the Serb Army,' he retorted that 'I probably added some "perhaps". Even today there is some "perhaps" about Srebrenica', with so much 'media manipulation that everyone who thinks for himself must be forced to reflect a little.'[59] Likewise, he continued to dismiss reports of former concentration camps in Bosnia as based 'on lies', and as propaganda, even long after credible evidence was available to the contrary.[60] As a diversion, Koštunica frequently focused instead on alleged NATO war crimes against the Serbs during the Kosovo War, and sought NATO's judicial prosecution.[61]

As a corollary, Koštunica evinced an early disdain for the International Criminal Tribunal for the former Yugoslavia and advised against cooperation with it, including in the matter of handing over indicted war criminals for trial. As he concluded in 1994, he saw the Tribunal as 'a political body, not a judicial institution,' and he doubted its impartiality, expressing his displeasure that similar courts had not been set up for 'much bloodier and bigger wars' in Vietnam and Afghanistan. In fact, the Tribunal was only 'the extended arm of a specific political orientation, representing the stick . . . and must simply exert pressure against the Serb side.'[62]

However, in a quintessentially Realpolitik approach, Koštunica believed that the international environment, despite its hostility to Serb interests, presented opportunities which could be seized. An indirect approach became increasingly attractive to Koštunica after the military defeats of 1995 when, in retrospect, he reassessed that in 1990–91 war had not been the best way to achieve goals, but that instead political means and the media could have been more effective.[63] In particular, according to Koštunica, the international community could be convinced to accept Serbian goals if only these were presented in the appropriate manner or, as he put it, by using 'a language which the West understands.'[64] On the contrary, he argued that the main problem up to now had been that the Serbs had presented their goals 'in a completely erroneous manner.'[65] As he saw it, the Serbs should have made a stronger political case earlier for their case, in order to convince the international community; arguing, that is, that 'the Serbs, with the collapse of Yugoslavia, cannot be deprived of what is guaranteed to other nations, namely the right to self-determination and their own state. That right, with respect to the Serb nation, cannot be fulfilled by stitching together, along the lines of the borders of the AVNOJ [post-World War II] republics of the former Yugoslavia. There is, therefore, political maneuver space to say that that goal [i.e. of a Serb state] is legitimate.'[66]

At the same time, increasingly cognizant of the balance of power, Koštunica was willing to achieve his goal of an expanded Serb state gradually, by phases, rather than trying to do so in one fell swoop. As he noted already in 1992, 'The political and cultural unity of Serbs within the area of the former Yugoslavia – which is one of the goals of the DSS [i.e. his political party] – can be achieved, of course, gradually, on condition that Serbia becomes a strong and democratic country.'[67] He emphasized that the goal of pursuing what he portrayed as a 'single democratic Serbian state' should be presented as not meaning that every single Serb live in it, nor that other 'national minorities' be not allowed. And, as he suggested, this goal could be achieved gradually and using political means: 'Neither is this pleading for such a state to be created immediately, nor that unification be achieved above all by war.'[68] By 1995, this piece-meal method for achieving a single Serbian state – that is Greater Serbia – had become his preferred strategy, as he suggested using the various peace plans being bandied about to facilitate 'a gradual integration of our ethnic and state space on the other side of the Drina [i.e. in Bosnia] with FR Yugoslavia.'[69]

Nevertheless, as he stressed (despite his somewhat opaque phrasing), he held that: 'Our goals are the same as those in 1992 – to support those forces in the Republika Srpska which strive for the maintenance of the Serbian nation as a political subject and for territorial continuity.'[70] What that meant was that he favored a distinct Serb political entity in Bosnia and that, in practical terms, one would have to redraw borders and force populations to move in order to facilitate the physical union of those territories with Serbia, since otherwise there was no possibility of creating his desired 'territorial continuity', given existing population patterns in Bosnia.

Who is to blame? Personalities and ideological values

Although loyalty to the nationalist cause has been a paramount consideration informing his paradigm, Koštunica's abiding aversion to the Left (represented by Milošević) and his identification of the Left with a betrayal of nationalist values, and his converse sympathy for the traditional Right (as represented, for example, by the SDS party of the Bosnian Serb leadership) arguably also colored his analytical approach and created a symbiosis between nationalist and political views. In many ways, Koštunica can be seen as the right-wing calque of Milošević's left-wing political bloc. Such ideological sympathies on Koštunica's part cannot be overlooked, as was highlighted by his positive response during a call-in radio program to a question about Dimitrije Ljotić (head of Serbia's fascist Rally party during the 1930s and 40s) and of the latter's ideology. According to Koštunica, Ljotić could not be reduced to the negative image which Yugoslavia's Communist regime had created of him. And, 'as for Ljotić's principles which you cite, it is hard for anyone who values morals not to agree with Ljotić's positions.'[71] Given the historical symbolism of someone like Ljotić for non-Serbs (and for many Serbs), this candid admission indicated both a nationalist blind-spot in Koštunica for making such a remark and, perhaps more seriously, suggested that he felt some affinity for nationalist and authoritarian ideologies such as those propagated by Ljotić.

Koštunica placed blame for not achieving nationalist goals squarely on Serbia's Communist (as he termed it) regime, and on Milošević in particular. As he calculated through his nationalist paradigm, one of the Communists' greatest failings was that they simply were not sincere nationalists: 'the Communists have never been nationalists in the enlightened, democratic, sense of the word, but only cynical nationalists – when required and only as much as required.'[72] In fact, asked whether Bosnian Serb leader Radovan Karadžić had made any mistakes, Koštunica responded that the only real one had been in trusting in Milošević's nationalism: 'There was, truth to say, a mistake linked with the assessment that one could rely on the national positions and the national interests of the regime in Belgrade . . . and that the [Milošević] regime was conducting a responsible national policy. He [i.e. Milošević] is . . . a cynical, not a true, nationalist.'[73] As Koštunica stressed, his greatest criticism of Milošević's regime was not the latter's monetary theft, which he expected simply 'because they are Communists', but rather 'the theft related to history, tradition, [and] national identity. That is what we cannot forget.'[74]

Indeed, perhaps the most serious criticism that Koštunica reserved for Milošević was that the latter had not been able to achieve nationalist goals because of an unsuccessful policy, not that he had selected inappropriate goals per se. For example, after the collapse of the RSK, Koštunica blamed Milošević not for having encouraged its creation in the first place through the use of violence and ethnic cleansing, but for not having supported it adequately. He termed Milošević's behavior 'the betrayal of the Republic of the Serbian Krajina' and anguished that: 'It is difficult to find an explanation for such a Pilate-like avoidance of moral and even legal obligations . . . in case of such aggression, it was understood that there were specific obligations on the part of the FR Yugoslavia. But FR Yugoslavia simply turned a deaf ear to such obligations.'[75] To be sure, Koštunica repeatedly also returned to criticism of Milošević for the latter's authoritarianism and corruption. However, Koštunica at the same time was effusive in his praise for the Bosnian Serb leadership, arguably every bit as authoritarian and corrupt as Milošević. Koštunica insisted, on the contrary, that the Bosnian Serb leaders governed in a fully democratic manner: 'That is not the usual form of responsibility, the usual form of relationship between a ruler and the people. Rather, that form of responsibility [is such] that the state rulers are under constant monitoring and pressure from the people.'[76] What appears to have been Koštunica's litmus test of acceptability was someone's stand on nationalism. While seeing himself as both a nationalist and a democrat, Koštunica's priorities clearly were in the first category. His justification for not joining the opposition Zajedno coalition which sought to oust Milošević in the winter of 1996–97, for example, was that the parties forming the latter believed, erroneously in his view, that 'the main question in the campaign must be social and economic issues.' On the contrary, 'the Democratic Party of Serbia held that the state and national issue is not an anachronism, but that in political and electoral struggles it is significant.'[77] As he concluded, 'Of course, the one who made the decisions, that is Slobodan Milošević, must now bear responsibility for the failures.'[78] Not only did Koštunica conveniently place all responsibility for Serbia's misery and failure solely on Milošević, but he also singled out the latter as the chief source of the international community's negative view of the Serbs, claiming that Milošević had come to represent the Serbs abroad. According to Koštunica, the international community's 'criterion . . . is completely simple and erroneous precisely because it is so simple. That [criterion] is Slobodan Milošević . . . [who] has become the litmus test for judging someone's political suitability. He is, according to the Americans, and as the entire smiling and rejuvenated international community echoes, the true yardstick for everything, the source and recourse of all political ideas among the Serbs, with the average Serb . . . willing to commit in his name the worst crimes.' In fact, Koštunica was angry that Milošević had usurped Serbian nationalism and had created in the West a negative image of the latter: 'You can be a completely average patriot, but if you are a Serb patriot, then according to the international community you are one of Milošević's men . . . all will be forgiven you if you only say that you are against Milošević.'[79]

Milošević's subsequent failure on Kosovo, likewise, attracted Koštunica's ire at a political rally in the run-up to the 24 September 2000 elections, when he blamed Milošević for 'isolation, sanctions, long lines, unrest, insecurity, uncertainty, last year's criminal airstrikes by NATO on our country . . . and the Kumanovo capitulation [i.e. the agreement ending the Kosovo War] which the Milošević regime proclaimed a victory.' And he added that Milošević would be unable to reverse that failure: 'Today we have someone else's foreign army and a foreign administration [in Kosovo]. Those who have brought them into Kosovo are not the ones to get them out.'[80] What was more, Koštunica was worried that under Milošević the rest of what he viewed as Serbian territories would literally perish: '[Republika] Srpska will be drowned in a unitary Bosnia-Herzegovina, and the remaining Serbian lands into some type of amorphous de-statified NATO mass. We deserve better.'[81]

Significantly, Koštunica's harsh criticism of Milošević on policy grounds did not extend to the Bosnian Serb regime. Typically, when asked whether the hard-core nationalist Bosnian Serb leader Radovan Karadžić had made mistakes, Koštunica rushed to his defense: 'All of us, of course, make mistakes. To be sure, there were some positions, some stands, which were, in my view, too sharp, and which should have been formulated otherwise or in a more gradual manner. However, I do not see that there is anything which I would call a basic error.'[82] Koštunica's admiration for Karadžić lasted even long after the latter had been removed from political life with his indictment for war crimes by the Tribunal, when Koštunica still complained that 'the legitimately-elected President [i.e. Karadžić] was replaced.'[83]

The impact of Koštunica's paradigm, with its emphasis on nationalist goals and values, extended also to the arena of domestic politics in Serbia. One can assume that this, in turn, also influenced directly the environment for conflict resolution negatively, since presumably a more open and democratic context characteristic of a civil society would have allowed for less extreme goals and a more inclusive negotiating framework. The criteria of democracy and, in particular, the civil society advocated by some individuals in Serbia were clearly subordinate to those of nationalism and the success or failure of achieving a Greater Serbia. Thus, Koštunica used the measure of commitment to nationalism, as he interpreted it, to attack not only Milošević but also the rest of the domestic political spectrum, accusing both – for different reasons – of not being sufficiently patriotic. He claimed that 'both the government and the champions of the so-called civil option' had an 'uncritical and worshipful position' toward the international community on nationalism, leading Serbia to a 'semi-colonial position.'[84]

Koštunica saw as his natural political allies not the democrats in Serbia so much as fellow-nationalists, however extreme. Thus, he favored creating an opposition coalition which would have included Vojislav Šešelj's Serbian Radical Party (Srpska radikalna stranka – SRS) and Nikola Rakitić's extremist Rally Party (Saborna stranka).[85] When an interviewer criticized Šešelj's SRS as having a platform based on 'national exclusivity, exemplary exclusion, and even primitivism,' Koštunica retorted that 'I would not agree with most of your evaluation of the SRS.'[86] On a practical plane, DSS officials had already cooperated with the SRS earlier in joint political rallies.[87] According to one of the DSS's vice-presidents, Koštunica had explained that his party had not entered into a coalition with Vojislav Šešelj's SRS only because the latter 'supported and maintained the [Milošević] regime. The SRS defended the national issue as it saw it from a narrow party perspective and not infrequently compromised it.'[88] That is, the sticking point had not been Šešelj's well-known extreme nationalism and brutal methods but his cooperation with Milošević. Likewise, Koštunica assessed that 'the closest party in terms of positions, political platform, and policy' to his own DSS was the hardline Bosnian Serb SDS party, as he told a caller on a radio program.[89]

Conversely, Koštunica disparaged the democratically-oriented Civic Alliance of Serbia (Građanski savez Srbije – GSS), which was a member of the opposition Zajedno movement, for what he alleged to be its 'a-national and, to a great extent, anti-national' outlook.[90] Elsewhere, he had accused the GSS, and even Vuk Drašković's right-wing nationalist SPO when the latter reduced its emphasis on nationalism, of having 'extremely a-national and even anti-national positions,' and characterized GSS leader Vesna Pešić, one of Serbia's most respected human rights advocates, as 'the leader of a marginal (but explicitly anti-Serb) party'.[91] Likewise, Koštunica quoted favorably a press article which characterized the Democratic Party led by Zoran Đinđić negatively as being 'midway between civic and pro-national, between pro-regime and anti-regime parties.'[92] Koštunica also accused Đinđić of acting 'in an extremely opportunistic manner' and of moving 'from an originally a-national position to a national one in terms of ties with the Republika Srpska, and then recently, in the last few months, back to an orientation which is a-national in everything and which in some things is close to the policy of the ruling party.'[93]

Indeed, Koštunica worried that 'some Serbs have lost their national identity, by becoming "Yugoslavs", "Europeans", "anti-nationalists", globalists, or else sub-national regionalists. The Serbs have a weakened national self-awareness, in addition to the perennial lack of self-discipline.'[94] As the September 2000 elections approached, Koštunica even fretted that Milošević might be replaced by some liberal party which would not defend nationalist positions adequately; or, as he put it, by 'some quisling parties with an uncritical stand toward America.'[95]

Resolving conflicts and the paradigm

In analysing and responding to specific concrete cases of conflict, Koštunica's views not surprisingly adhered closely to his overarching paradigm.

a) Bosnia-Herzegovina and Kosovo

In the case of Bosnia, Koštunica supported the efforts of the Serb Democratic Party (Srpska demokratska stranka – SDS), led by Radovan Karadžić, in setting up a Serb state in Bosnia- Herzegovina, which given the population patterns could be done only by the large-scale elimination of non-Serbs. For Koštunica, the Bosnian Serb leadership's goals were seen as legitimate: 'We assess, in fact, that the requests by the leadership of the Republika Srpska [i.e. the Bosnian Serb entity] at this stage are directed toward an objective which for us is legitimate and not debatable.'[96] For Koštunica, it was clear that the Bosnian Serbs 'cannot live together with the Muslims and Croats in the internationally-recognized state of Bosnia-Herzegovina. There is no reason whatsoever for us to force them to do that.'[97] And, he justified his own stand on Bosnia by arguing that the latter had never existed as a state and that, moreover, the intent of the Bosnians was to create 'an Islamic state on the territory of the entire Bosnia-Herzegovina.'[98] Asked whether he would go to Sarajevo to talk with the local population, including the Serbs who had stayed on in the city, Koštunica dismissed such a gesture by saying that: 'I did not feel a particular need to talk with people who are, simply, agents of Izetbegović's government.'[99]

His minimal condition for Bosnia was for a 'confederation of states, but not a confederated state. It seems to me that that is a perfectly natural and democratic solution.' It was clear that his intent was thereby to set up a temporary situation that would only postpone, and facilitate, rather than relinquish the goal of splitting off the areas of Bosnia controlled by the Serbs. As he asked rhetorically, 'Why not follow that path, why not facilitate a form of *temporary* [arrangement] which can last a certain number of years, a confederal state, that is a union of states, on that territory; and in a few years, that is in more tranquil conditions, the people then be empowered to declare in favor of integrating those two or three states [existing] on the territory of the former Bosnia-Herzegovina into a single state or in favor of independent states?' [emphasis in the original][100]

In particular, he was irked by Milošević's inability to gain more in Bosnia, which he attributed to a lack of skill in strategy. Asked if Milošević's ruling SPS party had implemented a suitable policy in Bosnia, Koštunica concluded: 'No, because of the simple fact that the issue was not presented in an appropriate manner. I think that the basic mistake was in not using all the aforementioned means – neither diplomatic nor media. That was not done in an appropriate manner . . . One cannot view it as an appropriate defense if particular arguments are not used sufficiently.'[101] For his part, Koštunica believed that a more subtle policy could achieve the desired goals more successfully despite the constraints of power. While existing agreements on Bosnia – such as the 1995 Dayton Accords – would have to be acknowledged, he nevertheless believed that they would not prove to be an insurmountable obstacle to achieving national goals. Thus, he suggested taking advantage of the Dayton Accords and the recognition of the Republika Srpska contained in that document in order to 'create a sort of Serbian political, cultural, and spiritual space' and to then 'strengthen ties between the Serbs which were severed in the second [i.e. post-World War II] Yugoslavia.'[102]

More precisely, as he told a radio audience in 1996: 'Put in a nutshell, the position of the Democratic Party of Serbia (DSS) on the Republika Srpska could be expressed in the following manner: While respecting the Dayton Accords as a fact of power rather than of justice and law, the DSS believes that everything must be done so that the Republika Srpska, that state within a foreign state – that is within Bosnia-Herzegovina – becomes as separate as possible, that it be as independent as possible, that it delineate as much as possible its attributes of statehood and, of course, that as strong relations as possible be again established between the

Republika Srpska and Serbia. When we speak of establishing those relations, we have in mind the fact that the Dayton Accords make possible such parallel special relations between the entities in Bosnia-Herzegovina and the neighboring states.'[103]

Koštunica, ever the realist, however added that the Serbs, as a weak force, would not be able to pursue their goals openly: 'Of course, as a small nation, in the circumstances in which we find ourselves, we cannot do what, let us say, the Germans in the Federal Republic of Germany did after World War II, proclaiming in their 1949 Constitution the union of West and East Germany as their national goal. We cannot do that.'

However, he continued by laying out his vision of enduring Serb policy goals and strategy *vis-à-vis* Bosnia: 'We must strive and aspire with all means toward the goal of uniting the Serbs on this and on the other side of the Drina, the two Serb states. That is our national goal. That is, in a certain way, similar to our national policy and our national goals before World War I when, despite the fact that Bosnia and Serbia were two distinct entities separated by a state boundary, they were viewed as closely linked. Jovan Dučić correctly wrote that Serbia and Bosnia are indivisible even in those days before 1914, when Bosnia was part of another country. We must follow that type of policy also today in the changed and different international circumstances, and this policy of the strongest possible linkages between Republika Srpska and the Federal Republic of Yugoslavia is the policy of the Democratic Party of Serbia. This [policy], of course, differs significantly from that of the prevailing [i.e. Milošević government] policy in Serbia and from the policy of certain opposition parties which support the integration of Republika Srpska into Bosnia-Herzegovina. Our policy is that of separating Republika Srpska and of bringing it closer to and unifying it with Serbia. We cannot and must not abandon that policy.'[104]

Before the military defeats of 1995, Koštunica suggested that Serb unity would be able to overcome pressure by the international community on the Serbs to accede to various peace plans provided that Milošević backed the Bosnian Serbs fully: 'We saw how that pressure ended up; if there is a united position by the Serbs from both this and the other side of the Drina, there is no pressure. The Contact Group's peace plan would not have lasted even for a few months if there had been a common united stand in Belgrade and Pale.'[105] He also suggested as a successful strategy that all the Serb entities unite to deal with the outside world, holding that it was necessary for 'Belgrade, Podgorica, Pale, and Knin to find a common political stand and that we go before the world with a united position,' through a 'Serb-Serb dialog.'[106]

When Milošević signed the Dayton Accords, Koštunica was predictably critical, labeling that 'a great political failure of the ruling regime,' in particular because he saw the 'independence of Republika Srpska as restricted' and condemned Milošević personally for having 'in practice slammed the door to any significant tie between FR Yugoslavia and the Republika Srpska.' Specifically, he castigated Milošević for not doing anything 'to enable the Bosnian Serbs to concretize at least part of the right to establish links with the mother country [i.e. Serbia].'[107] Koštunica interpreted Milošević's perceived coolness toward the Bosnian Serb leadership as particularly damning: 'the regime in Belgrade is attempting to push Republika Srpska away from itself and to reintegrate it into Bosnia-Herzegovina and in some way he shows greater interest for an integral Bosnia than for Republika Srpska'; he suggested instead that the 'special relations' allowed by the Dayton Accords should be emphasized.[108] At the same time, Koštunica believed that the West could be convinced to view the establishment of Republika Srpska's special relations with Serbia favorably by representing this as 'a pledge for peace in the region, which is in the interest of the Western countries.'[109]

Likewise, in the case of Kosovo, in consonance with his nationalist paradigm, the goal for Koštunica has been one of retaining the status quo as it was set – by Milošević – in 1989, with the suppression of Kosovo's autonomy. During the subsequent quiescent period which was characterized by harsh control by Belgrade and by peaceful protest by the Albanian community, Koštunica said little, apparently satisfied with the situation, and Kosovo attracted his attention only as the situation there heated up in the late 1990s.

Overall, he promoted the status quo insofar as he called for Kosovo's remaining within FRY, while however calling for refashioning Kosovo's interior borders in the interest of favoring control by the minority Serbian community: 'We have to consider something else – that the issue of Kosovo and Metohija be resolved for today and for tomorrow in a manner that (thanks to that "generosity") the latter remains within the structure of Yugoslavia. Let me be frank – why [should this be] within the framework of the present borders? Why should the borders not be changed in order to create compact Serb municipalities in Kosovo?'[110]

In line with that strategy, he opposed granting 'broad autonomy' for Kosovo, seeing that as a slippery slope, since 'that which is less than independence today can become independence tomorrow.'[111] As he saw it, the immediate threat was that: 'the Albanians insist on the territorialization of their collective rights – territorial autonomy, a federal entity, an independent Kosovo.' Instead, what he favored was for Kosovo to be integrated into Serbia – itself ostensibly to be regionalized like Spain – rather than creating an entity such as the Republika Srpska in Bosnia.[112] In order to facilitate Serb control over Kosovo, he proposed gerrymandering the province to further expand Serb control, and criticized Milošević's plans because these 'did not correct the borders of municipalities. By using that means, we could have a situation in which the majority of the Serb population lived in ethnically Serb municipalities and would thus be protected and more secure.' He also proposed 'a census and the checking of citizenship in Kosovo and Metohija' – long a Serb nationalist threat in preparation for the large-scale ouster of alleged Albanian immigrants.[113] At the same time, he opposed the ethnic councils proposed by the Milošević government for Kosovo. As he saw it, even though the proposed structure might hamstring the Albanian majority, it could also set a precedent for similar demands elsewhere, e.g. in Vojvodina or the Sandžak, by non-Serbs, and might therefore be harmful in the long term.[114]

The well-publicized 1998 photo of Koštunica in a Serb village in Kosovo holding an AK-47 assault rifle was not only symbolic, but perhaps also suggestive of his outlook.[115] Even when outwardly eschewing violence in favor of political means, what Koštunica viewed as the ideal policy for Kosovo was arguably a radical throwback to the past. Specifically, as he noted candidly on one occasion: 'The Kosovo issue was resolved in the first Yugoslavia [i.e. 1918–41] by political means, more or less successfully, including through the settlement of Kosovo by Serbs.'[116] Significantly, Serbia's policy during the interwar period, far from avoiding violence, had hinged on it – or at least the threat to use it. Interwar plans and policies had been characterized by campaigns of physical attack and fiscal and legal measures intended to force the Albanians to leave, culminating in the seizure of land and the government-supported settlement of Serbs on confiscated land, as well as by the drawing up of a plan to deport 400,000 Albanians to Turkey, which was derailed only by the approach of World War II.[117] Any such policy, even if considered mere wishful thinking, was likely to generate more violence and create more problems than it could solve – and would be a non-starter under any circumstances. As the situation between Belgrade and the international community deteriorated over Kosovo, however, Koštunica gauged the balance of power as heavily stacked against Serbia and assessed that Milošević precluded effective Serb resistance, which would be possible only 'under some better conditions, but not with the regime such as it.'[118] For good measure, he also criticized what he saw as Montenegro's unprincipled lack of support for Serbia's stand on Kosovo: 'if Serbia ends up without Kosovo, that will not torment Montenegro at the official level. This too shows how much the joint state is a façade and to what an extent it [i.e. FRY] is not even a state.'[119]

Once Belgrade had lost control over Kosovo to the international community in the aftermath of the 1999 Kosovo War, the parameters of the conflict, of course, were altered drastically. For Koštunica, the goal – that of retaining Kosovo – remained unchanged: 'For many of us, it is difficult to imagine Serbia without Kosovo.' And he thought this possible so long as the Serbs could retain a majority in northern Kosovo, apparently not concerned that this had been achieved only through ethnic cleansing.[120] However, the problem for Serbia presented itself now as one of coercion rather than deterrence, so far as the international community and the Albanians were concerned, with Belgrade playing a considerably weaker hand than before. Given NATO's overwhelming power, Koštunica now favored holding the line at the status quo for the time being (thus keeping Kosovo from moving toward independence), hoping to take advantage of opportunities as they arose once Milošević could be removed. He acknowledged that: 'With all their [i.e. NATO's] armada in Kosovo, it is difficult to change anything.' His proposal, therefore, was that: 'We must endeavor to maintain the status quo and look for an opportunity within the circumstances which will arise after the change of regime.'[121]

Russian President Vladimir Putin's visit to Belgrade and to Kosovo in June 2001 was instructive for the insights it provided on Koštunica's continuing rigidly traditional views on Kosovo, as he updated Putin on the local situation, since Putin's own statements presumably reflected his talks with Koštunica. Koštunica continued to portray for Putin's benefit the Albanian insurgents in the Preševo valley as 'terrorists' and blamed the international community for problems in Kosovo, while Putin assured his audience that: 'I agree completely with President Koštunica' and blamed the problems in Kosovo on 'national and religious intolerance and extremism' – i.e. on the Albanian side. Putin likewise repeated Koštunica's negative stance on the constitutional initiatives which UNMIK had introduced in Kosovo, as well as on planned elections.[122]

b) Regionalization
Over the years before coming to power, Koštunica consistently promoted what he called the regionalization of Serbia as a key component in his vision of conflict resolution, at least domestically. In an effort to promote this option, Koštunica portrayed it as the best way to enhance democracy while reinforcing cohesion: 'What is at stake is the idea of a project which has existed from the time when the DSS was founded. For me, regionalization is a formula by which the state democratizes and decentralizes itself, thereby preventing its own breakup'; one of its values is that 'you block

. . . separatist demands to break up that state.'[123] In order to garner support for regionalization, he often equated his plan with the internal restructuring in post-Franco Spain. However, in the latter case the intent had been to enable and institutionalize the expression of traditional ethnic and regional identities in such areas as Catalonia and the Basque country, while in Koštunica's vision the intent, on the contrary, appeared to be the opposite, as suggested by his above-mentioned intent to use his version of the Spanish model to integrate Kosovo into Serbia. As Koštunica stressed when making a case for Serbia's regionalization and the role of areas such as Kosovo, 'We are not in favor of their special status.'[124] He insisted that regionalization did not mean having existing units such as Vojvodina or the Sandžak as regions, but rather that there was a need to ensure that any new arrangement be 'from the point of view of Serbia'.[125]

In its essence, Koštunica's regionalization, equivalent to gerrymandering the entire country along new internal borders, could have been expected to do away with actual or potential demands for autonomy for minority areas, such as Kosovo, Vojvodina, the Sandžak, the Preševo valley, or even Montenegro, by refashioning Serbia's internal structure and eliminating traditional historically-based territorial entities, thus undermining traditional identities and making calls for autonomy by such entities more difficult. Rather than Spain, if anything Koštunica's plan is more reminiscent of interwar schemes to reconfigure Yugoslavia into a number of *banovine,* as a way to suppress historical identities and territories by using boundaries overlapping ethnic and historical units to reduce minority influence. Such regionalization is not likely to provide a structure for conflict resolution today that is any more successful than it was under the pre-war Yugoslav monarchy.

The Reality of Political Power and Paradigms

The new political environment – how much of a watershed?

Ultimately, how different is Koštunica from Milošević and how does the difference translate into prospects for conflict resolution now and in the future? The September 2000 elections and the ouster of Milošević from power the following month, which spelled the end of the Communist era, can rightly be viewed as a watershed in Serbian politics in many respects. The present government in Belgrade, whether at the federal or republic level, represents a notable step forward in virtually every area from the days of Milošević. That said, the direction and pace of change is not a purely academic question, since this will have an impact on how and whether conflicts are resolved. In the overlapping and sometimes confusing chains of responsibility within the new Yugoslav and Serbian governments, frequently mixed signals emerge, and it is not always clear who has influenced what policy. Yet, in order to understand Koštunica and his significance, it is important to seek to delineate his personal impact rather than conflating his role into that of the new government as a whole. As in the preceding section, an evaluation of Koštunica's policy statements, now supplemented by concrete policy initiatives made possible by his tenure in office, will serve as the basis for determining the extent of evolution and the implications for conflict. One cannot seek a strict parallelism between the two periods, not least because of the differences between the freedom of being in opposition and the responsibilities of being in power, with the need to deal with concrete issues as they present themselves. What should be sufficiently salient to determine the degree of evolution, however, is whether current declarations (including those by Koštunica's spokesmen, which one may assume reflect his own policy views) and actions reflect or contradict the earlier paradigm. Paradoxically, Koštunica is well-positioned to lead Serbia on the path to conflict resolution, given his solid credentials with traditional right-wing nationalists who might criticize more liberal elements wanting to compromise on nationalist positions. For example, Koštunica has been lionized by the Serb Orthodox Church, a bastion of nationalism for the past decade and a half, as one of the very few senior political figures who is a believer. The official Church newspaper, following his highly-publicized visit to the symbolic Serbian monastery at Mt Athos, enthused that 'such a strong relationship of a chief of our state with the Church has not existed for the past half century. When he came to Mt Athos, all the bells were rung in honor of the head of the mother state.'[126] Traditional nationalists have also endorsed him: Dobrica Ćosić, for example, calling him 'a proven patriot and a committed democrat . . . a man worthy of the people's trust.'[127]

But is it a paradigm shift?

In light of Koštunica's systematic and genuinely sincere paradigm, as outlined above, it would be a remarkable and welcome transformation if he had indeed abandoned abruptly views he had held for years up to the eve of the 2000 elections. It is, of course, difficult to change paradigms even over time, and Kuhn has compared the process of such a paradigm shift in the sciences to a revolution.[128] Paradigms are hard to dislodge even in the face of contradictory evidence, something that Jervis terms 'premature cognitive closure.' As Jervis notes, 'once a person has conceived of a problem in a given way, it is very hard to break out of his pattern of thought. New information, rather than calling the established sub-goal into question, will be interpreted within the old framework.'[129] As Jervis also concludes, decision-makers will naturally defend the paradigms they have adopted even when faced by dissonant information.[130] To be sure, a paradigm shift can also occur gradually, in an uneven and perhaps imperceptible fashion, rather than in one fell swoop or by formal fiat (although the latter means of proceeding might indeed be the clearest indication of genuine intent and have a decisive and immediate positive impact on conflict resolution in general). While difficult, such a paradigm shift, even in the Yugoslav context, is not out of the question, as illustrated by the basic shift in outlook and policy by Montenegro's current President Milo Đukanović, who matured from a hardline Serb nationalist to a leader exhibiting a much more inclusive and non-confrontational approach toward ethnic and religious-based conflicts.

The point at issue here is to determine to what extent Koštunica's nationalist paradigm, as outlined above, has changed with his coming to power. There is, understandably, a qualitative difference between being a political figure out of power and one in power. Individuals enjoying the relative luxury of promoting views in the vacuum of the theoretical world are suddenly confronted with having to match their beliefs and promises with the demands of having to make decisions, set goals, and craft and implement policy in the real world. Governing within any coalition, moreover, predictably places additional constraints even on ideologically-motivated leaders such as Koštunica, and the modicum of consensus required within such a political arrangement can be expected to affect not only policy choices but even the rhetoric, limiting the candid expressions of policy in public. In this respect, Koštunica has indeed muted some of his earlier more confrontational verbal representations of his beliefs, especially to foreign audiences.

A reassessment of methods

To be sure, Koštunica is certainly different from Milošević in important ways. It is perhaps in the area of methods in dealing with conflict that the differences between Koštunica and Milošević seem to be most clear-cut. Koštunica's new multilateral regional activism in some ways represents a departure, although even Milošević did maintain good relations with such neighbors as Romania, Bulgaria, Greece, Slovakia, and Hungary – although significantly not with Albania or with most of the other successor states of the former Yugoslavia. The fact that FRY under Milošević was not more involved in the regional and international arenas was not by choice (it would have been happy to be so), but because the international community intentionally isolated it as a way to express its displeasure with Milošević's policies. Likewise, Koštunica's visible readiness to sit down and talk with the international community and with regional neighbors, whether individually or in multi-state fora, in and of itself is a neutral act. After all, Milošević was also more than willing to negotiate deals (as had been Hitler at Munich). What is key instead is whether Koštunica sees such negotiations as a way to arrive at a genuine resolution of conflict, or on the contrary as a way to deflect unfavorable decisions, or even as the most feasible means by which to achieve traditional goals, especially in light of an inability to use more forceful means, as seen above. Koštunica has said as much in the past: that is, rather than confronting the international community, that it would be more effective to work with the latter to achieve the Serbs' nationalist goals. Cooperation with the international community was already a method proposed long ago as the most effective way to achieve Serbia's goals by getting the international community on its side, however unrealistic that might have been, given Serbia's goals of expansion. As Koštunica postulated in 1995, Milošević's mistake had been all along that 'instead of talking to the world he decided to fight against it. Thus, in the pursuit of state and national interests, we set off without clear goals and ended up with enemies instead of allies.'[131]

However, it may be in the readiness to use force where Koštunica, at least potentially, can represent the greatest break with the past. By temperament, conviction, and calculation,

Koštunica is averse to using methods such as Milošević's routine use of assassination of rivals and critics, or the latter's reliance on the Serb criminal element both as a political tool in conflicts and as an economic partner. Nor is Koštunica now as likely to launch wars to resolve disputes, certainly at this late juncture. In part, Koštunica's generally more realistic ability to weigh the correlation of forces than was the case with Milošević, who led Serbia into a series of unsuccessful wars, may deter him; although Koštunica's own insistence in the 1990s that the Croatian and Bosnian Serbs continue to defy the international community and their neighbors was clearly also a miscalculation and qualifies his current reluctance to have recourse to a military option. In particular, the lack of a popular reaction in Serbia to the collapse of the Croatian Serb entity in 1995 seemed to unsettle Koštunica, and to convince him that the military option was not always likely to be successful in achieving national goals, because of the changing military balance and the lack of Serb commitment to fighting for such goals. As he rued after the Serb defeat in the Krajina, 'Parties which try to include in their ranks all those who think nationalistically in a sober, enlightened, manner must be aware how difficult that is.'[132]

Koštunica clearly sees the balance of power today as tilted well away from Serbia: 'Today, we must adapt ourselves to the world such as it is. We must mend our wounds and rebuild our international ties, and we must respect reality, including that of the US's hegemonistic policy, which to a great extent has contributed to our people's grief.'[133] This is no small progress from Milošević's modus operandi, and in and of itself could have a positive impact on resolving conflicts. In concrete terms, for example, the outcome of such policy issues as Montenegro would no doubt have already played out differently, and probably more violently, under Milošević. Contrary to Koštunica's recourse to verbal threats and covert financial support for anti-independence parties, Milošević would very likely have envisioned the use of covert and overt violence on a significant scale to enforce Montenegro's subordination (and to ensure Milošević's own political position).

However, this does not mean that Koštunica categorically excludes the use of force. Significantly, it was Koštunica of all the figures in the government who was most reluctant to negotiate with the armed Albanian insurgents ('terrorists' as he called them) in the Preševo valley and who favored a military option.[134] In dealing with the Albanian insurgents there, Koštunica at the same time took a pragmatic approach, and was especially anxious to avoid what he termed 'something that would be reminiscent of the episode in Raçak,' that is the massacre in Kosovo 1998 which stiffened the stand of the international community; and he wanted to ensure that the authorities not be 'drawn into a provocation which could change the favorable international position of the country and lead to intervention from outside.'[135] The outcome of the implementation of the deal negotiated subsequently with the Preševo Albanian insurgents will be a major test of the extent of change in Koštunica's thinking in this respect. If the reintroduction of Serbian security forces there leads to a new environment in which all ethnic communities feel secure and are able to participate in decision-making, then this could pave the way for a peaceful resolution of the conflict and indicate a major change in Belgrade's approach. If, on the other hand, this leads to a reprise of the traditional harassment of non-Serb civilians and of the pressure intended to make them leave, even if this is done in a less crude manner than before, then the prospects for conflict resolution overall during Koštunica's presidency will not be encouraging.

Koštunica's negative perspective on representatives of other communities has also extended to his reluctance to talk to certain Albanian leaders in Kosovo, such as Hashim Thaqi. Whether genuinely believing his own rationale or not, Koštunica argued that now that FRY had become a 'democratically ordered state,' it was obliged to respect certain 'standards,' one of which is 'not negotiating with terrorists.' As he saw it, 'Would anyone in France or Spain agree to negotiate directly with terrorists? No, they would not. We would be acting irresponsibly not only toward ourselves but also toward others and toward the prevailing democratic position on terrorism if we agreed to negotiate with terrorists.'[136]

In general, however, Koštunica can be expected to refrain from the use of violence as readily to deal with conflicts, especially against fellow-Orthodox in, say, Vojvodina or Montenegro (which could also spark civil war, something that is anathema for Koštunica). Instead, he has opted for a greater emphasis on political means with respect to goals and has called for cooperation with the international community as a way to achieve these goals and, specifically, by convincing the latter that Serbia's goals are reasonable. He outlined his strategy for dealing with 'the world's leading nations' in his 2001 New Year's radio address: 'It is vital that we ourselves know what we want and that we be able to discuss and negotiate, and that we explain that our interests and theirs to a great extent can be compatible.'[137]

A reduced reliance on the military option will no doubt promote a more open and less confrontational atmosphere for some of the existing inter-state and internal conflicts and is a step forward. What may be of equal, if not greater, significance in this case than the methods Koštunica favors is his overarching paradigm and the goals which stem from that vision. Any compromises with reality need not be seen as contravening his basic original paradigm. As one could conclude from his own assessments and compromises in the face of force majeure in the past, Koštunica is very much a disciple of Realpolitik. While such realism affords him some flexibility, some experts in the field of conflict resolution have argued that such maximizing attitudes, wedded to achieving victory over perceived adversaries, may not be the most conducive approach to conflict resolution.[138] Given his legal training, it is perhaps not surprising that Koštunica places so much emphasis on a legalistic approach to issues related to conflict. However, his focus on legal principles can be glaringly selective. He has ignored, for example, Milošević's violent and legally dubious suppression of Vojvodina's and Kosovo's autonomy and the equally legally questionable transfer of the ownership of Kosovo's major public enterprises, such as the Trepča mining complex, to Serbia.

Although he prides himself on understanding the international community and on being able to make use of the rules of the game, Koštunica has shown on more than one occasion that he is not immune from miscalculating the balance of power, which for a practitioner of Realpolitik could have serious repercussions. For example, he has retained an exaggerated view of Serbia's importance, which could encourage him to misrepresent concessions by the international community. As he told an interviewer, 'our country has an exceptionally important place. I noticed an awareness of that in my talks with foreign officials. The Federal Republic of Yugoslavia is, in effect, a small Great Power.'[139]

However, key questions remain, such as whether Koštunica still believes in the eventual expansion of Serbia and in the latter's identity as a nationalist state in which the Serbs are the dominant nation; and, in practice, whether he will still work toward that end whenever he thinks this may be feasible, as with the annexation of at least the Serb-controlled entity in Bosnia and all or part of Kosovo, which would entail their partition and the promotion of a centralized Serbian state. In many ways, in fact, the possibility of partition of Bosnia and Kosovo may represent one of the biggest potential threats to regional stability currently, with implications far more far-reaching than, say, independence for Montenegro would have.

Such issues must be seen from the perspective of Koštunica's own paradigm. Proceeding from a reading of his assessments of conflicts over the years, one can conclude that he does operate on the basis of deeply-held, sincere beliefs that have been consistent and are probably difficult to compromise intellectually: what John Burton calls 'basic values that are not for trading.'[140] Koštunica himself has reiterated that he is sincere, that he is guided by principles, and that he is committed to consistency and continuity: 'If a person gives priority to principles, and I believe that my whole life I have given priority to principles . . . The position [of President] which I hold obligates me even more to follow the principles which I have followed even when I was not in power.'[141] All along, he has prided himself on the fact that his party was characterized by 'consistency' [*doslednost*] and that 'Nothing in our policy has changed.'[142]

In line with this thinking, Koštunica so far has not explicitly rejected any basic element of his earlier views, least of all the concept of Greater Serbia as a whole, which is in itself significant. Indeed, the DSS's official website continues – as of this writing – to display his party's unchanged platform, one of whose planks, as cited above, is the creation of a 'state . . . over the entire Serb ethnic space.' But what may be more crucial is whether he has at least done so implicitly; that is, whether he has ignored in practice his earlier paradigm by adopting goals and policies at variance with the latter. As of this writing, Koštunica has been in power only some ten months. Based on his admittedly lower-profile statements and on his policy decisions in the still evolving political arena, he appears to have retained much of his old central paradigm; and there are no indications up to now of a dramatic paradigm shift in the foreseeable future. Whatever compromises Koštunica may have had to make with more democratic elements within the Serbian polity in order to form what ultimately became the winning coalition, or with the international community in order to end Serbia's isolation, his political persona still seems to be guided basically by a personal penchant for traditional nationalism, tinged with an authoritarianism which overrides democratic tendencies. It is here that, to a disconcerting measure, Koštunica may share most visibly significant elements of Milošević's legacy. The goals, it can be argued, have often remained similar even when the strategies and methods have not.[143] And it is the goals – not only the methods – which will decide the prospects for conflict resolution. The partition of Bosnia or Kosovo, for example, even if accomplished by means of negotiations with the international community, would have the same impact as if done by force, not unlike the case of the 'negotiated' dismemberment of Czechoslovakia in 1938. What is more, such ostensibly non-violent 'solutions' could well be only a trigger for violence, as the aggrieved party seeks to resist. As the Prussian military philosopher Carl von Clausewitz noted insightfully, it is always the defender who starts a war by resisting a would-be aggressor, who would be satisfied achieving his goals by peaceful methods if possible.[144]

Assessing Indicators of Change

In order to find concrete indicators that will permit one to assess to what extent Koštunica's thinking has actually changed, we need to look at recent policy choices by the latter in concrete cases, such as Bosnia, FRY's internal structure, Montenegro or Kosovo.

Bosnia-Herzegovina

On Bosnia-Herzegovina, Koštunica's policy appears to continue to be shaped by what he still views as his duty and right to be involved with Serbs no matter where they live. As he put it, he has 'normal feelings for Serbs as fellow-nationals who live outside of Yugoslavia . . . There are special ties with those people, that is with Serbs who live in Bosnia-Herzegovina or in other former Yugoslav republics or in the diaspora. They are members of the same national community, and as President of Yugoslavia I have a special relationship with them.'[145] In the case of Bosnia, for example, once in power Koštunica was quick to show his support for the more nationalistic Bosnian Serb parties over more moderate forces in the run-up to the local elections.[146]

One of Koštunica's first policy initiatives with the victorious Bosnian Serb hardliners was to sign an agreement in March 2001 on 'special relations' in economic, political, and military fields. He not only missed an opportunity to counsel the hardliners in Bosnia to forgo their obstruction to reintegration and to allow the return of refugees to their homes, which would have enhanced stability; he thereby also promoted a hardening of Bosnian Serb positions and held out encouragement for an eventual partition and accession to Serbia. Although allowed originally by the Dayton Accords as a concession to the Serbs, the activation of such 'special relations' was by no means required. On the contrary, such measures can only contribute to a centrifugal process in Bosnia and could set the basis for future instability and the ignoring of basic human rights; they are likely to reinvigorate hardliners in all communities. There was no pressure on Koštunica to take this step (indeed, Croatia's President Stipe Mesić at the same time officially relinquished Croatia's equivalent right to special relations with the Bosnian Croat community); and Koštunica seems to have acted, on the contrary, with his earlier goals in mind. Koštunica explained thus his rationale for this initiative: 'what is close to my heart is the unity of Serbia and Montenegro and the strengthening of ties between FR Yugoslavia and Republika Srpska. I believe that this victory – and especially my own [victory] – in these elections in FR Yugoslavia will have an impact, and what an impact, on the situation in Republika Srpska. It will encourage the healthy and pure national forces, as well as the democratic ones, and to that effect a few days ago I had talks in Belgrade with Mirko Šarović of the SDS, Vice-President of Republika Srpska, and with Mr Mladen Ivanić, who is one of the new very influential politicians in the Republika Srpska, and who at the same time, as is true of our friends in the SDS, strives to combine something in policy which is national and democratic.'[147] While it remains to be seen to what extent and according to what timetable this agreement is implemented, even symbolic acts can provide insights into intent and can serve as the precursor of more concrete policies, as well as to encourage hardliners, as represented by the SDS (founded by Karadžić and now headed by Šarović) and by Ivanić's equally nationalistic Party of Democratic Progress.[148]

Paradoxically, the likelihood of cooperation between Bosnian Serb nationalist parties and Belgrade has improved with Milošević's ouster, since the latter – as a leftist – had had poor personal and ideological relations with the rightist nationalists in Bosnia, a situation which has changed completely with Koštunica, given the latter's pronounced right-wing sympathies.

Again on this issue, Koštunica's highly-publicized presence at the ceremonies in Trebinje, in the Serb-controlled part of Bosnia-Herzegovina, on the occasion of the reburial of Serb poet and nationalist activist Jovan Dučić (who had died in exile in the US during World War II and whose body was now being returned), stands out. The event, hosted by Bosnian Serb politicians and senior Orthodox clerics, predictably took on a distinctly religious-nationalist flavor, with Koštunica providing a ready foil for implied support from Serbia for local hardliners and a blurring of the border between Serbia and Serb-controlled areas in Bosnia-Herzegovina. The senior Orthodox clerics attending, indeed, prayed for 'our Christ-loving President Vojislav [Koštunica] and for the government of Republika Srpska,' and the occasion was treated as a state visit, with Koštunica reviewing an honor guard from the Bosnian Serb Army.[149] The solemn processions with Dučić's remains through Serb-controlled areas and the nationalist manifestations which they occasioned were eerily reminiscent of a similar series of processions of medieval Prince Lazar's bones used to rekindle Serbian nationalism in the late 1980s, and the symbolism would be readily apparent to local observers.[150]

If the Serb-controlled Krajina had not been reintegrated into Croatia by military means in 1995, and by subsequent negotiations in the case of eastern Slavonia, Koštunica would probably have a similar obstructive approach there now as he has had in relation to the Serbian entity in Bosnia, given his parallel support for the latter. Even so, Koštunica's foreign-policy adviser, Predrag Simić, has argued that Serbia should remain involved with Croatia's Serb minority community: 'Relations between Belgrade and Zagreb are pretty good, but we will have to insist on issues related to the Serbs' rights.'[151]

Internal structure of FRY

In general, the goals of maintaining FRY in its current territorial form, and preventing the emergence of greater autonomy for Serbia's constituent areas with significant minority populations, quickly became overriding needs in Koštunica's view, with not only the looming pro-independence moves by Montenegro, but also calls for autonomy (if not for outright independence) in Vojvodina, the Sandžak, and the Albanian-inhabited areas of southern Serbia, not to mention the continuing dilemma of Kosovo's status. Reacting to what he sees as negative centrifugal forces, Koštunica assured domestic audiences: 'I want to believe that . . . I will not be a new Gorbachev,' alluding to the break-up of the Soviet Union during the latter's term in office.[152]

Interestly, Koštunica appears to have quietly put into abeyance, at least for now, his earlier insistence on regionalization as a way to resolve conflict, perhaps out of concern for expected domestic opposition to such a plan or for its potential to fuel calls for genuine autonomy or independence.[153] However, although Koštunica now champions the cause of the sanctity of existing borders, this appears to be selective; while he now insists on this when it applies to cases such as Kosovo, the Muslim-majority Sandžak province, or Montenegro – all cases where it would benefit Serbia – he has not applied this principle to Bosnia-Herzegovina.[154]

Montenegro

In the case of Montenegro, during the run-up to the April 2001 elections, generally interpreted as a poll on the issue of independence, leaders in the Serbian/FRY political establishment were far from united, and that very disunity ensured that potential hardliners, such as Koštunica, would have to adopt a more realistic policy of acceptance, although he did so only grudgingly and often expressed himself in ambivalent and hostile terms. While Milošević had still been in power, Koštunica had advised the latter not to interfere with any planned referendum on independence and expressed a willingness to accept the results, despite his reservations on the wisdom of such a step.[155] Once in power, however, Koštunica's stand seems to have hardened, and his own eventual reluctant acceptance of whatever results emerged was soured by ominous warnings that the Montenegrin leadership would have to 'bear the responsibility for consequences for the region.'[156] One of Koštunica's basic fears has been that if Montenegro goes its own way, other areas would also seek greater autonomy or independence.[157] Koštunica's foreign-policy adviser, Predrag Simić, reinforced this practical reason for keeping FRY intact, noting that 'Serbia needs Yugoslavia because of Kosovo.' That is, if Montenegro were to become independent it would be that much harder for Belgrade to argue against Kosovo's independence.[158] Ironically, in order to cast doubt on the wisdom of independence for Montenegro, Koštunica even expressed a hollow concern that the Bosniaks living in the Sandžak, which was split between Serbia and Montenegro in 1945, would henceforth be divided between two separate states.[159] Seeking perhaps to undercut support for Montenegro abroad, Koštunica also expressed his suspicion that the referendum might not be fair and raised questions about whether there were more Montenegrins living in Montenegro or in Serbia. Of greater concern, he made veiled threats that in case Montenegro did opt for independence, then the Serb-controlled entity in Bosnia might also be justified in breaking away, not to speak of Macedonia's falling apart: 'Many countries in the area would begin to think: if one border changes, why would not some other also change, whether in the case of Macedonia or of Bosnia-Herzegovina?'[160]

In the event, anti-devolution DOS officials ended up in an alliance with Milošević's former followers in Montenegro, with both working to thwart Montenegrin efforts toward independence. Following the elections in which pro-independence forces garnered only a slight majority, the pro-FRY parties in Montenegro, although narrowly defeated and not part of Montenegro's government, were eager to work with the DOS on the federal status between Montenegro and Serbia.[161]

Kosovo

In the case of Kosovo, when he assumed power Koštunica found himself faced with a *de facto* absence of Yugoslav control over most of the territory, and with limited prospects of reestablishing the *status quo ante* or for solving the on-going problem within a framework acceptable to himself. At base, he sees the NATO presence as having 'initiated such changes as have awakened hopes for the independence of Kosovo – which we cannot accept!'[162] On the one hand, Koštunica has been anxious to assure foreign audiences of his good intentions toward Kosovo, for example telling Italian parliamentarians that: 'I am for . . . the essential autonomy of Kosovo in the Federal Republic of Yugoslavia – a truly multinational state with all human and minority rights.'[163] However, at the same time, there are indications of Koštunica's long-term intent to the effect that he would seek to reestablish, instead, as much of the *status quo ante* as possible in Kosovo, however unrealistic that might be; and that his goals have not changed greatly, although they might now have to be pursued gradually. Focusing on provisions of the operative UN Resolution 1244 which would favor his goals, he noted, for example, that: 'Our police must return to the security zone, while the Yugoslav Army must return to Kosovo, both of which are in concordance with Resolution 1244. It is only a matter of time.'[164] When asked in one domestic interview whether he was optimistic about a return of Belgrade's armed forces to Kosovo, Koštunica responded that: 'If you look at all the facts, then it is clear that at this moment this is hard to do. We know what the content of Resolution 1244 is and in what numbers and how the Yugoslav Army can return to Kosovo. With all these problems we are facing at the moment we cannot talk about that. However, the other side's, that is the international community's, obligations cannot be ignored. The situation in Kosovo and the return [of the Yugoslav Army] to Kosovo is an obligation for the other side.'[165]

The questionable decision by NATO allowing the return of FRY security forces to the buffer zone bordering on Kosovo can only be seen as a success by Koštunica, in that it is viewed in Belgrade as a step toward the return of a Serbian military presence in Kosovo itself. The fact that other organs of the FRY government, such as the Yugoslav Army, keep asserting such a goal without being corrected or disavowed by Koštunica must send a worrying message to the Albanians of Kosovo. For example, after the Yugoslav Army had returned to Sector B of the buffer zone, when General Nebojša Pavković, Chief of the General Staff, was asked whether it was now time to return also to Kosovo, he replied: 'statements by our government officials and by the representatives of the Coordinating Body indicate that there are discussions along those lines.'[166]

To be sure, Koštunica apparently realizes the limitations on Belgrade's options at the moment. In practical terms, he has been considerably more engaged in dealing with NATO and the UN on Kosovo than was true of Milošević, although the local Kosovo Serbs believe that the new government is still too preoccupied at home to devote enough attention to them. As Hans Haekkerup (Chief of the UN Mission in Kosovo) noted optimistically, Koštunica has been helpful in focusing on areas of common ground rather than on the 'hard problems,' and he was hopeful there would be agreement in such areas as elections in Kosovo, despite the fact that Koštunica had not yet committed himself.[167] However, Koštunica at the same time also seemed to be working on a different track. When the issue of setting up customs points along Kosovo's borders arose, Koštunica not unexpectedly opposed doing so along the Serbia-Kosovo border, while – as he wrote in a letter to Haekkerup – he wanted such customs points to be strengthened instead along the Kosovo-Macedonia and Kosovo-Albania borders, with direct FRY participation.[168] Koštunica's DSS party was adamant that customs collection could be a slippery slope, leading to Kosovo's own car license plates, passports and visas, and the establishment of state borders and of a state.[169]

Championing the *status quo* for now, a vice president of Koštunica's DSS, indeed, castigated more liberal Serbs for being willing to relinquish Kosovo: 'If such stands should become a majority, it is sure that Kosovo will no longer be an internal issue for this country, nor will the latter be asked anything when Kosovo is at issue.' He added: 'for now the most that we can do is to seek and demand from the international community to stop their daily ramblings in [seeking] a resolution to the Kosovo problem and instead to stick strictly to the legal framework for Kosmet, that is Resolution 1244.'[170]

Although Koštunica had had tense relations with pro-Milošević elements in Mitrovica during the 2000 election campaign, he also had close ties to some of the hardline paramilitary leaders in that area, including with the 'bridge watcher' paramilitary thugs running the Serb-controlled part of northern Kosovo. Indeed Marko Jakšić – who is a Vice-President of the DSS and the party's representative in Kosovo – is also head of the local Serb National Council (Srpsko narodno veće) which controls the Serb-held area and had close ties with paramilitary leaders, including with Oliver Ivanović, until the latter's ouster as a result of political infighting in June 2001.[171] When they set up roadblocks in April 2001 to protest the UN customs points, a representative of the Republic of Serbia came to express official support, including – as he put it – from Koštunica: 'I have come to bring you the unconditional support of the Government and Parliament of Serbia, the Federal Government and President Vojislav Koštunica for your legitimate and democratic resistance . . . Anyone who speaks differently must reflect on the harm that he brings to the Serb nation. The defense of national interests and the presence of the state of Serbia in this space are our priority goals.'[172] For a self-avowed legalist such as Koštunica to not only tolerate but encourage such supra-legal thug-centered parallel structures in the Serb-controlled part of Kosovo may appear counter-intuitive at first sight. However, the mission of the 'bridge watchers' to evict and prevent the return of the majority Albanian inhabitants of the northern part of Mitrovica (and to prevent the return of Serbs to the southern part of the city) has resulted in a successful separation of the two communities and of the two zones, and can be reconciled logically within Koštunica's broader nationalist paradigm.

The intent of Belgrade's engagement in Kosovo in general, and on the border points issue in particular, appeared to be to engineer a return of greater official involvement. DSS Vice-President Marko Jakšić demanded in a press conference that tax collection in Kosovo should be decided in direct negotiations between UNMIK and

Serbia's legal authorities, stating: 'The Kosovo Serbs are struggling to include the state organs of Serbia and Yugoslavia in the resolution of vital issues in the space where they have jurisdiction.'[173]

To be sure some local Serbs, with Koštunica's encouragement as well as that of the Belgrade authorities, have become more forthcoming in participating in the developing administrative arrangements for Kosovo under the auspices of the UN Mission. This too, however, should be viewed within the framework of Koštunica's own approach of using engagement as a means of participating in shaping the environment in order to attain traditional goals. Or, if the situation is heavily weighted against such an outcome, greater participation at the very least will enable Belgrade to obstruct and prevent a decisive outcome (such as *de facto* movement toward determining Kosovo's final status) that could preclude reaching Serb nationalist goals in the future. Thus Momčilo Trajković, President of the FRY team sent to participate in the negotiations for Kosovo, noted that in a meeting with Koštunica in April 2001: 'we reached an agreement on the [Yugoslav] federal state's joint approach in Kosovo and on the formation of a federal committee.' However, he also made it clear that the team would 'oppose energetically defining the status of Kosovo,' an attitude not likely to be helpful to basic progress in finding a solution.[174] Significantly, increased local Serb participation in Kosovo's Transitional Administrative Council has often hampered work toward even an interim administrative government structure for Kosovo. As the Serb representative, Rada Trajković, insisted, 'if you do not have mechanisms by which [autonomy] will be linked to Serbia and to Yugoslavia, this suggests even more strongly that it will be a very independent autonomy that will function without control.'[175]

In the past, when Serbia still controlled Kosovo, Koštunica had adamantly held to the position that all of Kosovo should remain part of Serbia.[176] He still appears to view the option of partition negatively, at least for now, although his reason may be that he is waiting for a better deal at a later date which would give the Serbs an even larger portion of Kosovo than that which they control at present.[177] However, a fall-back position – in the form of separation of the Serb and Albanian communities – at some time in the future does appear to be emerging within Yugoslav government circles. In particular, the negotiator for the Preševo issue, Nebojša Čović – a liberal within the Yugoslav government and probably acting as the main stalking horse for this initiative – by May 2001 was putting out feelers for such a territorial division of Kosovo. Although the proposal took the form of separate Serb and Albanian 'entities' within Kosovo, on the model of Bosnia, the subtext of the discourse was that such entities would be based on the *status quo* (or better), by which the Serbs retained control of the resource-rich North while leaving the majority Albanians the rest. While some in the government appear to view this as a permanent solution, those in Koštunica's circle seem to see this as a means to preclude a workable Kosovo and to retain Belgrade's influence, while preventing Kosovo's sovereignty and paving the way for an eventual reintegration of Kosovo within Serbia – however unrealistic that might be. In this vein Zoran Lutovac, a member of the FRY federal government's Team of Experts for National Minorities, noting that the Belgrade government now had only a limited opportunity to 'extract the maximum possible by means of an offensive and a wise policy,' suggested that the international community could end ethnic conflicts in the Balkans 'by shifting from multi-ethnic to ethnic concepts.' Specifically, Lutovac recommended setting up two separate entities in Kosovo, 'formalizing the current situation'. Asked if he thought this was possible, he replied: 'If Serbia strengthens its position, this proposal could be realistic.'[178] As Dragan Lazić, a member of the DSS's Central Council, further elucidated, the objective in Kosovo was to seek the 'optimal solution' given the current balance of forces. At the moment, according to Lazić, the best potential outcome was autonomy for the Serbs within Kosovo to the same degree that Kosovo would have autonomy within FRY. As Lazić noted, 'This does not exclude the variant of two entities based on the criterion of historical and ethnic rights', traditionally a position affirming the right of Serbs over territory both in cases where there is a Serb majority and (where there is no Serb majority) in cases where there can be a claim based on historical events. As Lazić assured: 'That option is the closest to the DSS and to President Koštunica.'[179]

Although any pre-partition entity-centered plan for Kosovo based on current lines of control could be taxed as being not only unjust (after all, the Albanians had made up more than 80 per cent of the population in the North, too, before being ethnically cleansed in 1999) and unworkable (given the experience with a similar set-up which the Serbs had engineered in Bosnia), its intent is fairly apparent as only a prelude to partition, by which the Serbs would gain disproportionately if unable to reestablish their earlier complete control over all of Kosovo.[180] Even a temporary configuration based on a Serb-controlled North plus various Serb-controlled enclaves throughout Kosovo would result in an unworkable and unstable situation by fragmenting Kosovo's economic, political, security, transportation, and territorial cohesion, and would thereby preclude any possibility of Kosovo's normal functioning. It is implausible, moreover, that partition would contribute to conflict resolution and stability in either Kosovo or Bosnia. Partition (particularly one where the Serbs essentially were allowed to select the territory they received) would not only result in mutilated and less viable rump Bosnian and Kosovar states, but the perceived viability of the underlying Serb ideology of territorial expansion and ethnically homogeneous states – and the success of its practitioners – very likely would fuel similar attempts at expansion by Serbia in the future, perhaps after the withdrawal of the international community's forces or a change in the international geo-political environment.

Indicative of Koštunica's intimate feelings on Kosovo is his discourse on the issue. On the one hand, he is prone to exaggerate on such questions as that of the numbers of Serb refugees.[181] What is more, the language he uses on occasion when speaking about Kosovo can be harsh and inflammatory, as was the case during a visit to Romania, when he called for a defense of Serbian cultural sites in Kosovo, which he claimed 'today are under an attack of ethnic and religious fanatics no less terrible than is the case in Afghanistan' (referring to the recent destruction of Buddhist statues there by the Taliban).[182] Revealingly, Koštunica told the Israeli press that he viewed Serbia's framework for approaching the

Albanian issue as analogous to that between Israel and the Palestinians – which is even more significant since by then the Intifada was well under way.[183] At the same time, Koštunica's foreign-policy adviser, Predrag Simić, has apparently been reinforcing with his boss the view that the Albanians are so indoctrinated with nationalism that there is now no point in negotiating with them.[184]

Confronting the Past as a Mirror of Conflict

Crime and punishment

A special indicator for measuring the extent of conceptual change – since it is an overarching factor which is intimately bound to the nationalist paradigm and, at the same time, crucial to conflict resolution with Serbia's neighbors – is that of coming to terms with the past and, in particular, with the war crimes which were one of the most painful parts of that past. In many ways, this issue may be a *sine qua non* for genuine conflict resolution. For Koštunica, the whole issue of war crimes, and the related cooperation with the Tribunal in The Hague, has been problematic and has had the potential of creating friction between him and the international community. Contrary to his portrayal of this as a marginal issue, this may instead be seen as being at the heart of past and of on-going conflicts and in many ways organic to the issue of the nationalist goal of establishing a Greater Serbia.

To be sure, Koštunica is on record as saying that in order for there to be inter-ethnic reconciliation: 'First it is vital and important for us to establish the truth, what really happened in the Balkans, and to attain an objective picture of events during the last few years.'[185] However, all indications are that his willingness to confront the past has continued to be connected, to a great extent, to his broader long-standing paradigm of justified nationalism and to his vision for the Serbian state, an approach that has evolved only slowly and to a limited extent over time. Typically, Koštunica was ready to blame 'much of the media which are distant from this country,' accusing them of 'behaving intolerantly and not objectively, with money and other circumstances playing their role,' as an explanation for the Serbs' negative image abroad.[186]

In particular, Koštunica has continued to deny that systematic war crimes and genocide often accompanied the implementation of Serb nationalist policy. When pressed, he has usually offered at best highly qualified and ambiguous evaluations of responsibility, even though he clearly had not been personally involved in any of the events in question. Koštunica, who has been reluctant to discuss the issue of war crimes at all, gave what was perhaps his clearest acknowledgment of war crimes committed in Kosovo (but there alone and completely centered only on Milošević) in an interview aired on the CBS television network's 60 Minutes II program (24 October 2000), when he said: 'For what Milošević did, and as a Serb, I will take responsibility for many of these crimes', at the same time adding the caveat: 'there are a lot of crimes on the other side and Serbs have been killed.' However, the following day Koštunica's staff hotly contested what he had supposedly said, claiming that the quote consisted of 'untrue words' and that it had been 'taken completely out of context.'[187]

Koštunica's general response, moreover, stands in stark contrast to that of Montenegro's President Milo Đukanović, who formally apologized to Croatia for Montenegro's role in the attacks against the latter in 1991. Instead, Koštunica has sought to muddle or emasculate the issue in a number of ways. For example, he has shifted blame for any war crimes, as in Kosovo, away from, as he put it, 'regular units, and least of all the Yugoslav Army' and onto paramilitary forces, that is putatively uncontrolled, unofficial, elements for whom the authorities – even Milošević – could not be held responsible.[188] Or Koštunica has sought to soften the impact of accusations of war crimes, claiming that 'most Albanians have returned [i.e. to Kosovo] and, according to my assessment, more have returned than had left.'[189] On other occasions, as an argument against the extradition of Milošević, he has claimed that: 'The war which was fought on the territory of the former Yugoslavia was difficult and took many lives, even though in part of the Western media there was of course an exaggeration as to the number of victims.'[190] At still other times, he has shifted the focus to NATO's alleged war crimes, principally during the 1999 Kosovo War, stating, for example: 'We are aware that a crime was committed; we will always repeat that NATO and the United States had the responsibility of evaluating the terrible consequences: the victims among the civilians, the damage to the infrastructure . . . No, the Serbs cannot forget; and I say that if the Serbs were to forget the bombings they would no longer be Serbs – they would lose their identity.'[191] Koštunica is likely to use such claims against NATO, in particular, to try to get political concessions. As he noted: 'Our state will not present a formal demand for compensation for war damages. The continuous reminding about that damage and about the political responsibility of those who carried out the air-strikes is stronger than any other form [of demand].'[192] One of his criticisms of the Tribunal, in fact, has been what he has called the 'Hague Prosecutor's avoidance of confronting NATO's war crimes.'[193]

On still other occasions, he has shifted the blame onto the victims, reiterating earlier claims that the Bosnian authorities had deliberately bombed their own people in order to elicit sympathy.[194] He also told a Serb audience that the Raçak massacre of Albanians in Kosovo, which had sparked an international reaction in 1998, had been 'a fabrication of a massacre.'[195] At best, he has frequently sought to divert responsibility by insisting on equal blame for all.[196] Reprising a traditional nationalist argument, he has even sought to link Serb suffering with that of the Jews, noting that both 'have a shared slavery and persecution . . . our suffering did not hurt much less.'[197] Elsewhere, as a diversion, Koštunica complained that there was no investigation of NATO 'war crimes', cast doubts on whether Bosnian Serb General Ratko Mladić (indicted for war crimes) had taken refuge in Serbia, and insisted that it was Serbia and FRY, instead, who were the victims. Koštunica has even sought huge compensation for the damage which NATO airstrikes caused, claiming that the NATO countries 'broke every rule of humanitarian law.'[198]

Koštunica's view of the Tribunal has not altered substantially over time, although the force of circumstances has often obliged him to modify his dealings with it. He has continued to allege that the Tribunal has a revenge-based mission and that it is characterized by 'selectivity,' claiming that only Serbs were being pursued. As he insisted, 'what is obvious here is that in this difficult war there were without a doubt victims and guilty on all sides . . . but, as we see, those [held] responsible are only on one side – the Serb side – and that is an additional reason against Milošević's extradition.'[199]

Instead of the Tribunal, Koštunica promoted the Truth and Reconciliation Committee, which he set up as a substitute for the Tribunal.[200] He also has taken refuge in legal casuistry, claiming that the FRY Constitution did not allow extradition of its citizens to the Tribunal, even though other Serbian politicians and legal scholars have dismissed such arguments.[201] Realistically, his on-going opposition to the Tribunal has had more to do with the fact that not only would individuals he no doubt considers Serb patriots also become liable to judicial procedures, but that even in the case of Milošević and of other leftist officials, public trials on charges of war crimes would likely also embarrass Koštunica's allies – senior members of the Serbian Orthodox Church, well-known nationalist intellectuals – and his political cohorts for their own previous direct involvement or support. What is perhaps far more important, such trials in an international forum could well discredit and delegitimize the ideology and practice of his type of hardline Serbian nationalism.

The extent of legal obfuscation perhaps was most striking in FRY's April 2001 request to the United Nations International Court of Justice (like the Tribunal, also based in The Hague) to dismiss the civil suit which the government of Bosnia-Herzegovina had brought in 1993 against the government of the Federal Republic of Yugoslavia on the charge of genocide. The FRY now argues that the case was invalid because today's FRY is not technically the legal successor of the pre-1991 Socialist Federative Republic of Yugoslavia (SFRY), so at the time the alleged crimes were committed it was neither a member of the United Nations nor a signatory of the UN's Genocide Convention.[202]

What to do with Milošević

Since coming to power, Koštunica's confrontation with the Tribunal has centered on the case of Milošević. Asked, as he was preparing to assume power, how he would react if the Tribunal exerted pressure to hand over Milošević, Koštunica was categorical: 'I will ignore them [i.e. such pressures] . . . I am encouraged in this by the fact that Europe is increasingly less insistent on that.' Instead, he again focused on the damage caused by NATO bombing.[203] When asked, once in power, about extraditing President Milošević, Koštunica told a *New York Times* interviewer that: 'It should never happen. I think that it's possible to do everything so that it should never happen . . . I must make compromises, but there is a line I cannot cross.'[204] He has also been known to argue that, as President, he simply did not have the power to hand over Milošević to the Tribunal: 'I am very surprised as to how much power is ascribed to me, and more so abroad than domestically . . . Those who today represent the democratic West . . . have forgotten a little what the president of a country can do.'[205]

The demands of political realism, to be sure, have obliged Koštunica to deal with the Tribunal's representatives, even though he portrayed the need to cooperate with the Tribunal very grudgingly: 'inevitable, since we have to survive.'[206] Predictably, he has had icy relations with the Tribunal's Chief Prosecutor, Carla Del Ponte, and repeatedly rejected her requests to hand over Milošević. When she visited in January 2001, she noted: 'It was impossible to have a dialog with President Vojislav Koštunica . . . He spoke for half an hour and accused the International Tribunal . . . I tried to inform him in a correct manner, but he did not want to listen to me.'[207] As Koštunica himself admitted, he had lectured the visiting Mrs Del Ponte about his views that the Tribunal was 'selective' in its prosecution and that 'selective justice is not justice.'[208]

For a long time, Koštunica was optimistic that the international community would eventually cede on this issue, believing that 'policy is now somewhat different' with a new Administration in

Washington.[209] However, yielding to political reality and to the split views within the ruling coalition, the FRY government had agreed by March 2001 to allow the Tribunal's Belgrade office to reopen and committed itself to cooperation in the areas of permitting on-site investigations, expelling those indicted who were not FRY citizens, and providing documents (although as of this writing apparently the latter has not happened). Over time, at least verbally, Koštunica himself was to become more cooperative, noting in April 2001: 'We are ready to cooperate with The Hague' – but injecting the caveat: 'that does not mean accepting everything that they seek', thus making the extent of Belgrade's commitment to cooperate still unclear.[210] Significantly, in Koštunica's understanding, cooperating with the Tribunal had come to mean something specific, as in providing the latter with documents about alleged war crimes against the Serbs.[211] By April 2001, nevertheless, Belgrade had committed itself to serving Milošević with the Tribunal indictment and arrest warrant which Mrs Del Ponte had first delivered to the Serbian and FRY authorities in January 2001, and this was carried out in May.

Perhaps no single issue has been as controversial as the decision to arrest Milošević (and other former officials), and the choice of whether to try him in Belgrade on charges of corruption and the misuse of power, as Koštunica preferred, or at The Hague, as the Tribunal and Koštunica's rivals in Belgrade preferred. The simple arrest of Milošević seemed to be the ideal solution for Koštunica at the time, not only deflating demands by the international community for Milošević's immediate extradition to The Hague and guaranteeing the flow of foreign aid, but also serving to dismantle the leftist ruling system which Koštunica despises on ideological grounds (albeit from a right-wing perspective), while side-stepping the more embarrassing issue of war crimes, which would also cause dissonance for Koštunica's prevalent paradigm. At the same time, as of April 2001, Koštunica was still insisting that 'The Hague is not in my thoughts . . . Cooperation with the Hague Tribunal does not mean accepting everything and trampling national dignity for a few dollars.'[212] Asked about how Koštunica felt about cooperating with the Tribunal, DSS Vice-President

Dragan Mašrićanin noted: 'I personally believe that for him [i.e. Koštunica] that issue even now is far from being in the front row.'[213]

Koštunica may have believed that passing the law was enough for the moment, and that he could continue the more effective route of delay and passive resistance as opposed to outright refusal. According to Mašrićanin: 'In order for us to show that we are cooperating, it is more than enough to enact the law on cooperation,' suggesting that there was still a readiness in Koštunica's immediate circle to substitute form for substance on this issue. Asked if Koštunica had promised to extradite Milošević by the end of the summer, Mašrićanin hotly denied such an intention: 'As far as I know, I can say that this is a plain stupidity.'[214] Koštunica, for his part, originally believed that 'even if Milošević had not been arrested, the US Administration would still have continued to help Yugoslavia.'[215]

In the end mounting international pressure – and the prospects of losing foreign aid which was to be decided at the Donors' Conference in Brussels on 29 June and the later Paris Group meeting to reprogram FRY's debts – led to a decree allowing extradition and then to Milošević's extradition just before that deadline. However, this apparently was only accomplished by spiriting Milošević out of the country and by bypassing Koštunica, using the Republic of Serbia to issue the decree and then Serbia's assets and chain of command rather than the FRY ones under Koštunica's jurisdiction to carry out the operation. Expecting that the decree's legality would be contested in the courts over a long period of time, Koštunica even until the end of June still seemed confident that Milošević would not be extradited.[216] Significantly, Koštunica's heated negative reaction to the sudden extradition, accompanied by his claim that not only had he been opposed to the action but that he had not even been informed of it, reflected a continuing traditional approach on his part.[217] Even if Koštunica did know, as some in the government have suggested, his repeated insistence that he did not is troubling, in that it suggests at the very least a willingness on his part to hinder such procedures in the future and to use the issue to gain political leverage against members of his own coalition.[218]

In opposition to the Tribunal, Koštunica had favored his own Truth and Reconciliation Commission, which he had established on 29 March 2001 with an envisioned three-year lifespan: a mechanism to deal with the recent past as a substitute for more extensive cooperation with the Tribunal, and which appeared to conform to his original paradigm. Not only was it limited to citizens from FRY (Serbia) and apparently numbered only one non-Serb among its members, begging the question of who was to be reconciled to whom, but there was no provision to call any witnesses. The mandate and structure of the Commission suggested an attempt at 'damage control' rather than genuine conflict resolution.[219] Rather than a genuine healing process of fact-finding and apportioning responsibility, as had been the case in South Africa, in Serbia on the contrary the process appeared to augur an academic discussion destined to produce an anodyne finding in favor of allocating equal political responsibility and victimization to all communities, in order thereby to dilute what Koštunica has consistently viewed as the unfair assigning of principal responsibility to Serbian actors. Some of the members appointed cast a further shadow on the results that could be expected from the Commission, since they included such individuals as Darko Tanasković, an academic who had been one of the most hawkish propagandists against the Muslims, and Radovan Bigović, an Orthodox cleric who had played a similar negative role with his view of non-Serbs. Conversely, two prominent members, Latinka Perović and Vojin Dimitrijević, resigned early in the process, citing the inherent limitations set on the Commission's terms of reference.

Milošević as the problem

It has become convenient in Serbia nowadays to blame everything on Milošević. As Koštunica noted: 'Up until 5 October, it was easy: Slobodan Milošević was guilty of everything. His policy was unreasonable and inflexible, he lacked vision, he was not able to see the next step, he was completely divorced from reality, lacked a strategic goal, and did not understand national interests.'[220] Not surprisingly, Koštunica's explanation for the cause of Serbia's alienation from the international community has focused largely on Milošević, with Milošević personally portrayed as the problem. Immediately after the 2000 elections, Koštunica was confident that once Milošević was ousted, Serbia's problems with the international community would end, thereby ignoring the fact that, rather than the individual in power, it was the aggressive nationalist policies which Milošević had pursued which were responsible for Serbia's isolation and for the failed wars.[221]

However, affixing all responsibility for past 'errors' to an individual, and a leftist one to boot (anathema as such to Koštunica), was convenient, since this made it possible to avoid calling into question Koštunica's own underlying nationalist ideology. On the contrary, Koštunica was anxious to draw a sharp distinction between Milošević and Serbian nationalism, placing all blame on the former and concluding that Milošević's nationalism was not the real thing: 'We now have come to what is the people's mood and what is the true measure of something which is attributed to the Serbs, that is nationalism. That nationalism does not exist. When that whole story was over, when the entire misfortune had ended, one could see that much of that was manipulation by Milošević, that his policy was in fact cynical nationalism in which the national [element] is used only as a way to reach and remain in power.'[222]

While Milošević's personal leadership role certainly was decisive in determining policy in most key areas, nevertheless it would be erroneous to see him as having operated in a vacuum and to gloss over the support for ultranationalist goals and policies – and often for incitement far outpacing Milošević's own agenda – by leaders in the Serbian Orthodox Church, intellectual circles, the Army, and in most of the opposition parties, especially at key junctures as Yugoslavia disintegrated. Indeed, such a facile assessment threatens to distort the historical record and to drive future policy in a negative direction. Although Koštunica has identified the problem as Milošević personally, one can argue that the more basic problem is really that of the traditional goal of establishing a Greater Serbia, no matter who champions it. Political amnesia, while perhaps intellectually comforting, is an unsound basis for a new beginning; and unless this recent past is addressed in a forthright manner, a genuine transformation of the political environment in Serbia favoring successful conflict resolution may be delayed, if not derailed. Koštunica is perfectly willing to use and maximize the inheritance from Milošević's policy where convenient, as in Bosnia-Herzegovina: namely, the Serb entity which was established by force and ethnic cleansing. The impression is that Koštunica would also like to preserve the centralized Serbia created by the suppression of Vojvodina's and Kosovo's autonomy (although in the latter case this has been overcome by events), which Milošević engineered in 1989.

In fact, Vojvodina's status is likely to increase as a contentious issue. Sentiment for a return of the pre-1989 autonomy and even for status as a separate republic has been strong in Vojvodina, but has met with little sympathy or willingness to engage on the issue on the part of Koštunica. While non-Serb communities represent a substantial percentage of Vojvodina's population, the divide with Serbia is not predominantly ethnic; many of the leaders and a significant proportion of the support for autonomy come also from within Vojvodina's Serb community, where the sense of economic exploitation and political dictates from Belgrade contribute to fueling calls for autonomy.[223] Relations between Koštunica and some leaders from Vojvodina by early 2001 had become increasingly acrimonious, with one leader, Nenad Čanak (himself within the DOS coalition), accusing Koštunica of being a 'Greater Serbian'.[224]

The DOS coalition is itself divided on this issue, with Đindić's Democratic Party, for example, more flexible, and willing to accept such autonomy.[225] In order to deflect moves toward autonomy, Koštunica's DSS, on the contrary, has even been willing to work at the local level in Vojvodina with such parties such as Milošević's SPS and the Party of Serb Unity, which the late paramilitary chief Arkan founded.[226] Significantly, when Koštunica picked someone as the DSS's vice-president responsible for affairs in Vojvodina, it was Goran Bulajić, someone opposed to Vojvodina's increased autonomy.[227]

Prospects for the Future

Given the early indications of Koštunica's decision-making, what are the prospects for conflict and for conflict resolution? If Koštunica's paradigm is genuine, as appears to be the case, his personal ability to jettison or even relax his positions may be restricted indeed, even as the verbal and political maneuvering has increased in intensity, and he may be hard put to avert conflict before it reaches serious levels. In particular, a practical implication of his rigid analytical framework may well be that the prospects for Koštunica's contributing to what Sandole calls 'provention' of a conflict, or 'prevention . . . by removing its causes, and by creating conditions in which it cannot occur', may continue to be limited at best.[228]

A civil society?

However, one area of potential domestic change which could have a dramatic impact on conflict resolution by inducing a paradigm shift would be the emergence of a civil society in Serbia. The open and inclusive environment reflective of a civil society would likely be more conducive than an authoritarian one – which is closed to a constructive and realistic dialog – to conflict resolution, and could be effective in putting rigid nationalistic paradigms to rest. Promoting a civil society makes all the more sense in an ethnically plural society such as Serbia's. If, on the contrary, democratic values continue to be subordinated to nationalist ones, then the process of conflict resolution may remain complicated and unsure. Koštunica's position on developing a civil society, however, remains ambivalent at best and the prospects are not very encouraging. To be sure, Koštunica has sought to allay foreign fears about his brand of nationalism, portraying it in benign terms: 'In my case, nationalism means a constant control and a continuous preoccupation for what happens to my people, without excluding other peoples. I am interested only in the fate of the Serbs . . . My nationalism is defensive and benevolent toward other peoples, especially if one compares it to that aggressive one which has imperialist pretensions and which extends also to other countries.'[229] However, any evolution in respect to his earlier perceived balance between nationalism and democracy in favor of the latter seems to be modest so far, as suggested by his visit to Russia immediately after assuming office in October 2000, when he hinted at his understanding of democracy. In a telling observation, Koštunica singled out 'the later Solzhenitsyn' – a figure characterized in his later years by a distinctly illiberal, xenophobic, and ultranationalistic outlook – as a great contemporary thinker. What is more, on that occasion Koštunica assured his hosts that he saw both Soviet Communism and liberal Western democracy in equally negative terms, and portrayed the US and the former Soviet Union as morally and politically equivalent when he stressed that he shared Solzhenitsyn's disillusionment with 20th-century totalitarian societies, 'both Soviet and American.'[230] For Koštunica, in fact, the US embodies 'democratic totalitarianism', imposing its views worldwide not only in material but also in moral terms.[231]

Likewise at home, glimpses of Koštunica's outlook raise concerns. For example, reacting to Corax [Predrag Koraksić], Serbia's leading political cartoonist, who had satirized him, Koštunica placed the incident in a darkly unpatriotic context: 'Behind that approach I am afraid that there is hidden a secret glorification of all that exists across the ocean and scorn for all that exists in our country. Much of the harm in our country is generated from abroad and it seems to me that this would be an interesting topic for Corax's pen [instead].'[232] Significantly, Koštunica has continued to view former Bosnian Serb leader

Radovan Karadžić as primarily a democrat.[233] Perhaps more ominously, Koštunica's negative reaction to non-government organizations [NGOs] might be a worrying indication for the future of democratic development. As he noted, in discussing human-rights NGOs in the US, which he alleges are obstructing the new US Administration's policy, 'When it is a question of our [NGOs], the situation is completely different [than in the US] and here you have many, very many organizations which in many respects remind one of associations which must exist, which fulfill important duties, but on the other hand you have those which are simply branches or sections of those in America about which I spoke. My criticism was directed only to that type of NGO, not to all.'[234] Koštunica again vented his spleen with NGOs before the DSS Central Council, when he spoke against 'militant well-heeled non-government organizations,' accusing them of wanting to 'write history or to determine history for money.'[235] And, when asked whether he could envisage his DSS and Milošević's SPS joining in a coalition government, Koštunica noted that such things were possible.[236]

On a related front, Koštunica in his new post has gone out of his way to highlight publicly his own and Serbia's special linkages with the Serbian Orthodox Church, including with some of the more hardline elements in the Church, which may well leave out a significant proportion of the population. For example, when he visited the hawkish cleric Metropolitan Amfilohije Radović (who happens to be his brother-in-law) in Montenegro soon after assuming office, he stressed that: 'I came, as always, for spiritual advice, and for political advice . . . I entered these elections with the blessing of Metropolitan Amfilohije.'[237] Not coincidentally, Koštunica took Metropolitan Amfilohije along as part of his retinue on his official trip to Moscow following the 2000 elections. The DSS's political platform, significantly, still sees a close interrelationship between Serbian Orthodoxy and the Serbian national identity: 'In support of that goal [i.e. to eliminate a perceived spiritual void and national indifference], religious education must be introduced, without ideological prejudice, into the schools and the Serbian Orthodox Church must again have that position which it has always had in the history of our nation.'[238]

Constraints of the political environment

In the short term at least, the current domestic and regional political environment may make it difficult for Koštunica to implement policies meant to achieve maximalist goals, at least as long as the international community is also prepared to remain actively engaged in the region. This of itself may blunt the impact of his policy toward conflicts. This does not mean, however, that more limited gains – which could contribute to the attainment one day of greater goals and which are consonant with Koštunica's traditional paradigm – are not possible. Encouragingly, there are already some built-in domestic and international mechanisms which may limit Koštunica's ability to implement policies as he would like, even though their effectiveness and durability cannot be predicted.

First, Koštunica will likely find it difficult to translate objectives based on his current paradigm into policy, given the current balance of forces between Serbia and the international community – provided the latter maintains a consensus and a robust presence on the ground. This inability to challenge the international community will be the case especially because of Serbia's reliance on foreign economic aid, and because of its desire for political reintegration – needs which are not likely to change in the foreseeable future. To be sure, Koštunica would like to reduce this limiting factor. For example, thinking very much in balance-of-power terms, he would like to have Europe and Russia play a bigger political role in the region in order to balance the United States and to use any splits in the international community, especially within Europe and between the latter and the United States, in order to increase his room for maneuver. As he told one interviewer: 'Cooperation with Europe suits Yugoslavia. Our policy should be pro-European and it should rely on cooperation with Russia . . . The Russian Federation . . . in this part of the European expanse . . . can represent a counterweight to the

American monopoly. Taking into account that America has a predominant influence in NATO, our foreign-policy priority should be cooperation with Europe . . . joining the "Partnership for Peace" would be a direction of a kind for us, a compromise solution within which our country should move, to be "East to the West, and West to the East".'[239]

Likewise, in a transparent attempt to foster differences between Italy and the US, Koštunica told an Italian audience that Italy understands the Balkans better than the US, and also noted that: 'The Federal Republic of Yugoslavia expects more from Europe than from America.'[240] However, realistically, this is a very unsure hope, and cooperation with the international community as a whole is likely to be necessary. In order to gain the latter's support, Koštunica has emphasized those concepts which he believes will have a resonance abroad. One such theme is the assurance that Serbia can be a factor for stability: 'Serbia will be one of the main guarantors of stability in this area of the Balkans.'[241]

Secondly, Koštunica will find that most Serbs are simply tired of war and its consequences – and would view open war with particular distaste – a factor which has been a source of disappointment to nationalists all along since 1991 and which is likely only to be more pronounced nowadays and for the foreseeable future. Moreover, some of the potential conflicts – such as those revolving around Montenegro and Vojvodina – involve other Serbs or Orthodox communities, which could produce dissonance in Koštunica's view of the Serbs as pitted against hostile non-Serb forces.

Thirdly, Koštunica does not wield anywhere near the power that Milošević did after the latter had consolidated his position. Instead, the present FRY and Serbian governments are still based on an uneasy coalition, and the other two principal power clusters in the government can be expected to dampen at least some of the more extreme policies that Koštunica might otherwise attempt based on his own assessments. The genuinely democratic GSS and other figures in the DOS coalition such as Nenad Čanak are likely to do so on principle, while Đindić's DS will likely be motivated by pragmatic considerations and by long-standing political competition with Koštunica and the latter's DSS party. Indications of disagreements over policymaking have surfaced on several occasions, including over the handing over in March 2001 of Milomir Stakić, a Serb suspect (but a Bosnian citizen), to the Tribunal to face charges of war crimes. Koštunica, in an apparent slap at rival coalition member Đinđić (reputed to favor such extraditions), complained on this occasion that he had not known about the extradition and that such a step was 'an exception which should not have been made.'[242]

Differences over how to deal with Vojvodina, Montenegro, and the Albanians in southern Serbia can also be discerned between Koštunica and some of his more liberal or pragmatic coalition partners. For example, in relation to the March 2001 arrest of Milošević, Koštunica took the opportunity to hurl some thinly-veiled criticism of how his coalition partners had carried out the operation, in which he claimed 'there were errors,' and promising that it would be determined 'who is responsible' for those errors. On this occasion, in another implicit criticism of some of his more cooperative coalition partners, Koštunica stressed that Milošević would not be handed over to the Tribunal, which he alleged carried out only 'selective justice.'[243]

However, in another sense, the presence of the coalition government at the same time also provides Koštunica with greater maneuvering room *vis-à-vis* the international community, by creating, whether intentionally or not, a 'good cop, bad cop' environment, with liberals in the coalition presenting alternative views or 'explaining' Koštunica's stands and motivations in a more favorable light to foreign audiences. This softened image of Koštunica dilutes the more accurate negative impression which the latter, if he had exclusive power, might create abroad and distorts the corrective feedback that he might otherwise receive. Ultimately, internal policy differences notwithstanding, Koštunica's negative input acts to neutralize a good part of the liberals' efforts, insofar as the environment for conflict resolution is concerned; and liberals in Serbia themselves have criticized Koštunica for his hardline nationalist stands.

What is more, there is no guarantee that the present political balance in Belgrade will remain unaltered. There were strong indications throughout early 2001 that there would be new elections either in Serbia or FRY or in both, with an increasingly confident DSS being the main promoter of a new round of voting.[244] Significantly, as of April 2001, opinion polls in Serbia indicated that Koštunica was far and away the most popular political figure, raising the possibility that in future elections he might be able to consolidate his position by jettisoning his more liberal or pragmatic rivals, some of whom he has already overshadowed. The controversy surrounding the extradition of Milošević highlighted the long-standing simmering ideological and personal rifts within the coalition government between the liberals and pragmatists in one camp and Koštunica and supporters of the old regime in the other. Clearly the momentum for extradition had come from Koštunica's rivals within the government, including Ðinđić, probably motivated not only by the need for foreign aid but also by seeing this step as a means to gain status with the international community at Koštunica's expense, especially after the latter's own success abroad. The undercurrents of political rivalry had also been stoked by the May 2001 exposé in the Croatian press of cigarette black-marketing, implicating Ðinđić and Montenegro's President Ðukanović. No matter who was behind the leak to the media, such reports served to tarnish the reputation and erode the ability to attract votes of two of Koštunica's main rivals, and to facilitate the consolidation of power by Koštunica.[245] There had already been early subtle moves to discredit Ðinđić, such as that by the editor of the Belgrade daily *Blic* and reputed Koštunica confidant Miodrag Ðuričić, who had accused Ðinđić of 'being considered Germany's man' and who spoke ominously of 'a German protectorate.'[246] In the wake of the post-extradition mutual recriminations, Koštunica and his DSS party appeared poised to seek political advantage, calling for a restructuring of the Serbian and FRY governments and becoming more insistent on greater political identity and influence for the DSS.[247]

If and when Montenegro should become independent, leaving only Serbia, or if Koštunica should become dominant on the political scene without the 'ballast' of the more liberal partners of his coalition, one could reasonably expect him to start expressing his traditional views more freely and perhaps to be less accommodating than he has been. Even within the short term, the constant in-fighting between Đindić and Koštunica, in particular, is likely to come to a head over some aspect of personality and power, and one cannot predict whether this would lead Koštunica to become so consumed by the power struggle that he would be forced to forgo a hard line in dealing with other conflicts, or whether it would tempt him to press his nationalist agenda even more vigorously in order to mobilize domestic support, including among former Milošević supporters in the electorate.[248]

While his rivalry with coalition partner Đindić may limit Koštunica's room for maneuver as long as the coalition lasts, out of concern that Đindić might garner the international community's sympathies should Koštunica be seen to be too rigid, Koštunica's own success abroad at times may have caused Đindić to come around to some of Koštunica's positions in order to avoid being bypassed, especially in cases where, unlike that of the extradition of Milošević, there appeared to be little support forthcoming from abroad for alternative approaches. In fact, at an earlier stage, Đindić himself had retreated from his earlier calls to extradite Milošević immediately and, perhaps unnerved by the apparent acceptance of Koštunica abroad despite his opposition, had pronounced himself also in favor of trying Milošević first at home.[249] While the rivalry may often be more personal than ideological, with Đindić himself going out of his way recently to stress that: 'Our differences are essentially minor . . . in ideological terms our goals are similar,' the potential for basic differences in policy choices based on this rivalry remains a significant factor.[250]

Conclusion

If anything, this case study underlines the persistence of paradigms as leaders grapple with decision-making; the importance of such frameworks in influencing, in this case, conflict resolution, and the corollary importance of changing dysfunctional paradigms if there is to be progress. If Koštunica's current paradigm is not conducive to conflict resolution, what might induce him to deviate in a way that might generate greater flexibility and thus facilitate conflict resolution, or at least help avert new conflicts in the absence of the emergence of a civil society? And, in that light, how might the international community contribute to such a process, which would provide more solid guarantees of reduced tensions and instability? Given the close correlation between paradigms and policy, the feedback from concrete results would probably have the greatest impact in leading to modifications in the paradigm. In other words, the failure of policies based on his paradigms would probably be the single most effective means to induce President Koštunica to reassess those paradigms. Ultimately, for any statesman the value of theory can be measured by its success or failure in the unforgiving arena of the real world. A practitioner of statecraft is likely to gauge the validity of a paradigm by its utility in enabling him to analyse, forecast, and make correct decisions. In the realm of conflict – as is also true in the natural sciences – success can be expected to reinforce a prevailing paradigm, while the dissonance generated by failure can be decisive in triggering revaluation and change. As Kuhn posited for the natural sciences, 'Failure of existing rules is the prelude to a search for new ones.'[251]

Perhaps pushing Koštunica in the right direction in stages through modulated negative , as well as positive, feedback might be the most successful strategy. There is, one must remember, a difference in the functioning of paradigms in human conflict and in the natural sciences, where paradigms can be applied to inert problems. Human conflict, on the contrary, as Clausewitz pointed out for the phenomenon of war, consists of a contest between independent wills, resulting in a dynamic which depends on this irreplicable interaction and can be influenced consciously by other human players. That is, rather than feedback being inert and impersonal, in human conflict it can be tailored specifically to affect another player's policies and thus, indirectly, his overarching paradigm. Specifically, an active rather than a passive role on the part of the international community, intended to provide guidance to Koštunica in the form of concrete policy feedback, could substantially shape his operational environment, and thereby speed up the process of altering his basic paradigm and the policy decisions which flow from the latter. Any time gained by the international community in this process would be no small gain, since delays encouraged by the latter's dilatory policy, as seen in the case of its dealing with Bosnia, only postpones a solution and, in the process, can harden existing positions, thus further complicating what at an early stage may yet be a malleable situation.

The progress made so far on cooperation with the Tribunal may serve as a road-map for how to encourage Koštunica to change, or at the very least to prevent him from implementing his preferred policy options. Consistent pressure by the international community, in other words, can generate at least piece-meal concessions from Koštunica and promote movement in the right direction, by relying on his political realism and, perhaps more importantly, on the readiness of more liberal and pragmatic elements in the government to cooperate in pressuring him.

At some point, such incremental and piece-meal quantitative changes may add up disproportionately into qualitative change. In other words, the compromises which Koštunica may have to accept as a result of domestic political fragmentation and international pressure could add up to a point where the incremental steps which these compromises represent lead to geometric change, translating into a genuine transformation in Koštunica's basic paradigm, and thereby herald a break with the past and a new environment more appropriate to conflict resolution.[252] Moreover, such a trend would further encourage liberal elements in the Serbian polity who have a different concept of how to identify and eliminate the causes of conflict and who would have the all-important empathy to ensure, as Richard E. Rubenstein puts it, that 'all parties' basic human needs be satisfied.'[253]

Koštunica can be expected to cooperate with the international community based on two considerations: if he feels that doing so will support goals consistent with his paradigm, or if he cannot avoid doing so. For the international community, the primary criterion should be whether each of Koštunica's – and its own – moves favors or hinders an eventual change in Koštunica's paradigm to the benefit of an environment more welcoming to conflict resolution. Establishing overlapping linkages with Koštunica might encourage him to think and act in a more moderate fashion over time, in effect 'Gulliverizing' or limiting his scope of action by relying on numerous mutually reinforcing material and political links that he might be loath to jeopardize. This appears to have been the thinking behind the benefits which the international community quickly extended to the new government in Belgrade. However, such an outcome is not automatic. A multiplicity of such linkages could work almost as easily to Koštunica's advantage, if the process reintegrates Serbia fully into the international community before genuine change is institutionalized. Belgrade's systematic pursuit of new or renewed membership in international and regional political and economic bodies, and even in NATO's Partnership for Peace, need not be viewed in Belgrade as being in conflict with traditional goals. Rather Koštunica, rightly or wrongly, may view such reintegration into international bodies as facilitating his pursuit of traditional goals by diplomatic means, especially by dissolving international opposition. For such a strategy toward Koštunica to be effective, the international community has to be engaged actively and systematically, rather than seeking the easy short-term option while making irretrievable concessions along the way. Given changing international attitudes and a growing sense of fatigue with involvement in the Balkans, it might be very difficult indeed to recreate even the basic consensus needed to undo such steps by reimposing economic or political sanctions, or even to generate meaningful pressure at a considerably lower level. Koštunica has been remarkably successful in reintegrating FRY into most international political and financial bodies already, despite still unresolved issues such as that of cooperation with the Tribunal. Foreign leverage is thus diminishing rapidly.[254]

The engineering of a paradigm shift is by no means an automatic or assured result. Indeed, such a process is fragile and uneven, and in this case dependent on continuing pressure, unity of purpose, and commitment on the part of the international community. Conversely, concessions by the latter, motivated by a desire for easier short-term outcomes, could prove counterproductive for the long run. Perceived foreign weakness or indifference in the face of Koštunica's hardline policies and any perceived success on his part would strengthen Koštunica at the expense of more liberal elements and facilitate the imposition of his agenda on the coalition as a whole. As Sandole underlines, success can serve as 'positive reinforcement' for existing perceptions; and 'as this "response generalization" occurs over time, it will be progressively more difficult to undermine that internalized x-y connection, even in cases where it no longer applies.'[255]

Success for Koštunica's traditional goals – if he were allowed to outmaneuver the Tribunal, or if he could engineer the return of a Serb security presence in Kosovo or a *de facto* partition of Bosnia or Kosovo – would, if anything, confirm his existing views, enhance his domestic political position, make him less amenable to conflict resolution, and fuel further forays along this line in the future. In his self-assessment, his measure of success so far may have been limited to that of reestablishing Serbia's image, which he believes has proceeded unexpectedly quickly.[256] Not surprisingly, Koštunica represented his May 2001 visit to the United States as successful and as support for his policy.[257] And extravagant attention and approval by the international community could be seen within Koštunica's circle as approval for FRY's President personally, enhancing the legitimacy of his views.[258] However, even the hope of more concrete gains, such as the suggestion by Lord Owen (former European Union negotiator for ex-Yugoslavia) that it might be advisable to 'compensate' Serbia with territory in Bosnia if Kosovo became independent, would probably only encourage someone like Koštunica to think that the international community might eventually accept the partition of Bosnia in Serbia's favor and would encourage him to hold out.[259]

In sum, based on the evidence available, one may conclude that Koštunica's record on conflict resolution is so far mixed at best, and that his evolution since assuming power, rather than a paradigm shift, represents a natural transition from earlier positions now shaped by the realities and constraints of domestic political concerns and by international relations. As was the case with other conservatives – such as President Richard Nixon in initiating US–China relations or Prime Minister Menachem Begin's deal with Egypt – Koštunica could take the major steps necessary for reconciliation, provided he wants to do so. That intent, however, is still not apparent. In many ways, Koštunica still represents an obstacle to further progress. To a significant extent, much of the initiative for the progress made up to now can be attributed to the liberals in the DOS coalition, while Koštunica by contrast has often been a drag on change and on measures helpful to conflict resolution. In the end, unless the Belgrade government tackles the legacy of traditional Great Serbian nationalism early, this will make it easier for the latter to persist and to become institutionalized through what is at present an inchoate process of rehabilitation. At the same time, an unwillingness or inability to face the recent past and its relationship to that ideology will continue to shape current policy and affect prospects for conflict resolution negatively. In many ways Serbia remains a mini-empire, with non-Serb populations in areas annexed as a result of the 1912–13 Balkans Wars (Sandžak), World War I (the Bulgarian areas attached to eastern Serbia), and World War II (Vojvodina, including eastern Srijem which was transferred from Croatia), and with the Preševo valley transferred to Serbia in the 1960s from Kosovo, not to speak of the additional complicating factors of Montenegro and Kosovo. Given the ethnic diversity not just of FRY but also of Serbia itself, anything short of significant movement toward the establishment of a civil society and the genuine abandonment of a Greater Serbian nationalist paradigm is unlikely to result in the preconditions necessary for collaborative problem-solving, which is the hallmark of conflict resolution. In the absence of progress in the latter domain, genuine change and stability are likely to remain elusive.

Ultimately and more broadly, this study of President Koštunica should reaffirm the importance of being aware of and addressing basic paradigms when embarking on conflict resolution. Unless the underlying analytical frameworks of participants are assessed accurately and taken into account, it is unlikely that outsiders will appreciate how the participants understand a conflict and what their objectives are. Conversely, to be aware of a participant's paradigm can provide what may be crucial insights into the latter's thinking and allow third parties to shape strategies to guide participants in a direction which will facilitate conflict resolution.

Notes

1. The DSS is part of the Democratic Opposition of Serbia (DOS) coalition, encompassing three main political clusters – Koštunica's own DSS, the Democratic Party (Demokratska stranka – DS) headed by Zoran Đinđić, and the Civic Alliance of Serbia (Građanski savez Srbije – GSS), and another fifteen smaller parties.

2. For the differences in terminology and an insightful overview of the concepts, see Dennis J. D. Sandole, 'Paradigms, theories, and metaphors in conflict and conflict resolution: coherence or confusion?' in Dennis J. D. Sandole and Hugo van der Merwe (eds), *Conflict Resolution Theory and Practice; Integration and Application* (Manchester: Manchester University Press, 1993), pp. 3–24.

3. See Thomas S. Kuhn, *The Structure of Scientific Revolutions* (Chicago: Chicago University Press, 3rd edn 1996). This work was first published in 1962.

4. Robert Jervis, *Perception and Misperception in International Politics* (Princeton: Princeton University Press, 1976).

5. As Sandole notes perceptively, paradigms influence a 'different sense of problems appropriate to that thing and of methods relevant to solving them,' 'Paradigms, theories, and metaphors in conflict and conflict resolution,' p. 3. Indeed, Young Back Choi has equated paradigms to 'guides for action' that, as such, have a predictive value, *Paradigms and Conventions; Uncertainty, Decision Making, and Entrepreneurship* (Ann Arbor: University of Michigan Press, 1993), pp. 37–8.

6. Kuhn, p. 15.

7. Richard K. Betts, 'Analysis, war, and decisions: why intelligence failures are inevitable', *World Politics*, v. 31 (October 1978), pp. 83–4.

8. Richard E. Rubenstein, *Conflict Resolution and Power Politics; Global Conflict after the Cold War*, ICAR Working Paper (Fairfax, Virginia: George Mason University, January 1996), pp. 2–3.

9. John Burton, *Resolving Deep-Rooted Conflicts: A Handbook* (Lanham, Maryland: University Press of America, 1987), p. 21.

10. Dennis J. D. Sandole, *Capturing the Complexity of Conflict; Dealing with Violent Ethnic Conflicts of the Post-War Era* (London and New York: Pinter, 1999), p. 18.

11. In fact, highlighting the personal concentration of decision-making, one of Koštunica's advisers, Slobodan Samardžić, assessed that 'there is a much greater number of requests to meet with [Koštunica], but I think it is not good that many things which could be decided at the level of government agencies are decided at the level of the President of the [Yugoslav] Republic. Simply put, people must become accustomed for institutions to begin to function.' Interview with Slobodan Samardžić by Olga Nikolić, 'Kosovo nije Hirošima' [Kosovo is not Hiroshima], *Glas javnosti* (Belgrade), 14 January 2001, online at URL: http://arhiva.glas-javnosti.co.yu/arhiva/2001/01/14/srpski/I01011301.shtm

12. Typically, even a villager was quoted as welcoming Koštunica to power because 'Someone from Serbia will take much better care of Serbia than someone from anywhere else.' Danica Kirka, 'Koštunica remains a mystery to most Yugoslavs,' *Washington Times*, 29 October 2000, p. C10.

13. See the interview with Zorica Radović (Mrs Koštunica) by Radmila Stanković, 'Nisam prva dama' [I am not the First Lady], *NIN*, 28 December 2000, p. 32.

14. Koštunica quoted in Miroslav Mikuljanac, 'Pravda iz novinskog članka' [Truth from a newspaper article], *Borba*, 13 August 1992, p. 11. At the time, the Democratic Party, complained that the similar name for Koštunica's DSS was an attempt to exploit the DS's popularity and would confuse voters.

15. The DSS's view of its emergence as a separate party is taken from the DSS's official website at
    URL: http://www.dss.org.yu/prikazi. asp?rubrika=15

16. On the intellectual and historical development of Serbia's national ideology, see Branimir Anzulović, *Heavenly Serbia; From Myth to Genocide* (New York: New York University Press, 1999); and Ivo Banac, *The National Question in Yugoslavia; Origins, History, Politics* (Ithaca, New York: Cornell University Press, 1984), pp. 141–225.

17. Interview with Vojislav Koštunica by Mirjana Bobić-Mojsilović, 'Jedno srpsko ne i jedno srpsko da' [A Serbian no and a Serbian yes], *Duga* (Belgrade), 13–19 May 1995, pp. 18–19. This was, of course, not true, since the Croats, Albanians, and Bosniaks also all lived in a number of republics after 1945.

18. *Duga*, 13–19 May 1995, p. 19. In fact, the Serb majority in Vojvodina had only been engineered thanks to the mass expulsion of the German, and to a lesser extent the Hungarian, community, and then to large-scale

settlement of Serbs after 1945; the lands of Vojvodina had never been part of Serbia.

19. Vojislav Koštunica, 'Protiv despotije' [Against despotism], *NIN* (Belgrade), 28 July 1995, p. 20.

20. Interview with Vojislav Koštunica by Predrag Popović, 'Veći je revolt među Beograđanima izazvalo ponašanje navijača na prvenstvu Evrope u Grčkoj, nego pad RSK' [The behavior of the fans at the European championships triggered a greater revolt among the population of Belgrade than did the fall of the RSK], *Argument* (Belgrade), 14 August 1995, pp. 8–9.

21. Interview with Vojislav Koštunica by Vesna Bjekić, 'Cilj je smena vlasti' [The goal is to change the government], *Spona* (Frankfurt), 16 December 1993, p. 11.

22. Interview with Vojislav Koštunica by Zorica Stanivuković, 'Izbori, pa podela vlasti' [Elections, and then a division of power], *Evropski Ekspres* (Frankfurt), 18 November 1993, p. 5. (*Evropski Ekspres* was the foreign edition of the Belgrade daily *Politika Ekspres*.)

23. *Argument*, 14 August 1995, p. 8.

24. *Argument*, 14 August 1995, p. 8.

25. The DSS party platform, crafted in 1992, was still carried on the party's official website as of June 2001, online at
    URL: http://www.dss.org.yu/prikazi.asp?rubrika=16

26. Interview with Mirko Petrović, DSS Vice-President and President of the Executive Council of the DSS, by Predrag Popović, 'DSS je autentična opoziciona stranka na koju ovaj režim ne može da računa' [The DSS is an authentic opposition party on which the regime cannot count], *Argument*, 17 June 1995, p. 7.

27. See the DSS party platform, online at
    URL: http://www.dss.org.yu/prikazi.asp?rubrika=16

28. *NIN*, 28 July 1995, p. 20.

29. *NIN*, 28 July 1995, p. 20.

30. *Spona*, 16 December 1993, p. 11.

31. All quotes from the interview with Vojislav Koštunica by Ljiljana Begenišić, 'Nacija i demokracija' [Nation and democracy], *Javnost* (Pale), 26 October 1996, p. 13.

32. Interview with Vojislav Koštunica by M. Gligorijević, 'Protiv sejanja magle' [Against the sowing of confusion], *NIN*, 21 March 1997, p. 17.

33. *Javnost*, 26 October 1996, p. 13.

34. Interview with Vojislav Koštunica by Milivoje Glišić, 'Petokraka s ružom' [Red star with a rose], *NIN*, 2 December 1994, p. 17.

35. *Spona*, 16 December 1993, p. 11.

36. *NIN*, 28 July 1995, p. 20.

37. *NIN*, 28 July 1995, p. 20.

38. According to the 1991 census, only 60.4 per cent of the population of Serbia (including Vojvodina and Kosovo) were Serbs, and even that figure was likely to be inflated, given the chronic undercounting of the Roma, who for statistical purposes are often lumped in the Serb category. Instead of the official 70,126 in Serbia proper, Serb ethnic experts estimated the true number of Roma to be between 500,000 and a million, thereby also diminishing proportionately the number of statistical Serbs by a corresponding proportion. See Miroljub Jevtić, 'Drumovi će poželeti Srba' [The roads will miss the Serbs], *Duga*, 20 August-2 September 1994, p. 96.

39. See the interview with Zorica Radović (Mrs Koštunica) by Radmila Stanković, 'Nisam prva dama' [I am not the First Lady], *NIN*, 28 December 2000, p. 32.

40. *NIN*, 28 July 1995, p. 20.

41. *Javnost*, 26 October 1996, p. 14.

42. Interview with Vojislav Koštunica by Batić Bačević, 'Američka veza' [American link], *NIN*, 25 February 1999, p. 21.

43. *Argument*, 14 August 1995, p. 8.

44. *Spona*, 16 December 1993, p. 11.

45. Interview with Vojislav Koštunica by Nataša Mijušković, 'U novi vek s uređenom državom' [Into the new century with an orderly state], *Glas javnosti*, 8 December 2000, online at
URL: www.glas-javnosti.co.yu/danas/srpski/I00120701.shtm

46. Interview with Vojislav Koštunica by S. N., 'Šljiva s nanom' [Plum with mint], *NIN*, 10 August 2000, p. 15.

47. Interview with Vojislav Koštunica by Mirjana Mitrović, 'Dr Vojislav Koštunica o onima koji stalno menjaju stavove' [Dr Vojislav Koštunica on those who continuously change their positions], *Duga*, 11–24 September 1999, p. 9.

48. Interview with Vojislav Koštunica by Dragan Bisenić, 'After the first verdict,' *Ha'aretz* (Tel Aviv), 26 November 2000, online at
URL: http://www3.haaretz.co.il/eng/scripts/print.asp?id=101941

49. *Glas javnosti*, 8 December 2000.

50. Interview with Vojislav Koštunica by Nenad Stefanović, 'Branićemo pobedu' [We will defend our victory], *Vreme* (Belgrade), 20 September 2000, online at
URL: http://www.vreme.com/507/4.htm

51. *Argument*, 14 August 1995, p. 8.

52. Interview with Vojislav Koštunica by Nenad Stefanović, 'Sudbonosna godina' [Crucial year], *Vreme International* (Belgrade), 17 February 1996, p. 17; and interview with Vojislav Koštunica by Luka Mičetić,

'Opsednutost demokratijom' [Besieged by democracy], *NIN*, 2 August 1996, p. 12.

53. Interview with Vojislav Koštunica by Stevan Nikšić, 'Branićemo svaki glas' [We will defend every vote], *NIN*, 21 September 2000, p. 20.

54. *NIN*, 2 December 1994, p. 17.

55. *Javnost*, 26 October 1996, p. 15.

56. *Javnost*, 26 October 1996, p. 15.

57. Vojislav Koštunica, 'Protiv despotije' [Against despotism], *NIN*, 28 July 1995, p. 21

58. *Duga*, 13–19 May 1995, p. 22.

59. *Vreme International*, 17 February 1996, p. 18.

60. Interview with Vojislav Koštunica by Tomo Kuzmanović, 'Režim potcenjuje humanitarni problem' [The regime underestimates the humanitarian problem], *Duga*, 12–25 September 1998, p. 8.

61. For example, in the interview in *Vreme*, 20 September 2000.

62. *Duga*, 13–19 May 1995, p. 21.

63. *Vreme International*, 17 February 1996, p. 18.

64. *NIN*, 2 December 1994, p. 16.

65. *NIN*, 2 December 1994, p. 16.

66. *NIN*, 2 December 1994, p. 16.

67. Interview with Vojislav Koštunica by Miroslav Mikuljanac, 'Pravda iz novinskog članka' [Truth from a newspaper article], *Borba* (Belgrade), 13 August 1992, p. 11.

68. *NIN*, 2 December 1994, p. 17.

69. *Argument*, 14 August 1995, p. 8.

70. *Vreme International*, 17 February 1996, p. 18.

71. Dated 2 December 1996, text available online on the official DSS website at URL: http://www.dss.org.yu/arhiva/intervju96.html
      Ljotić was a key official of Serbia's collaborationist government which withdrew with the Germans after the Soviet Army and the Partisans took Belgrade in October 1944, and subsequently helped run a Serbian government-in-exile under German auspices. For a history of his movement, see Mladen Stefanović, *Zbor Dimitrija Ljotića 1934–1945* [Dimitrije Ljotić's Rally 1934–1945] (Belgrade: Narodna knjiga, 1984).

72. *NIN*, 28 July 1995, p. 20.

73. *NIN*, 2 December 1994, p. 17.

74. *NIN*, 21 March 1997, p. 15.

75. *Argument*, 14 August 1995, p. 8.

76. *Duga*, 13–19 May 1995, p. 20.

77. *NIN*, 21 March 1997, p. 15.

78. *Argument*, 14 August 1995, p. 9.

79. Interview with Vojislav Koštunica, 'Zaslužujemo bolje' [We deserve better], *Nezavisne novine* (Banja Luka), 16 June 2000, online at URL: http://www.trebinje.com/cgi-bin/printthis.cgi?page=426

80. Rally of 20 September 2000, text online on Free Serbia website at URL: http://www.xs4all.nl/~freeserb/specials/broadcasts/20092000

81. *Nezavisne novine*, 16 June 2000.

82. *NIN*, 2 December 1994, p. 17.

83. *Nezavisne novine*, 16 June 2000.

84. *NIN*, 28 July 1995, p. 20.

85. *Javnost*, 26 October 1996, p. 13.

86. *NIN*, 2 August 1996, p. 12.

87. *Argument*, 17 June 1995, p. 7.

88. *NIN*, 21 March 1997, p. 15.

89. Radio program, 4 December 1996, text available online on the DSS's official website at URL: http://www.dss.org.yu/arhiva/intervju96.html

90. *NIN*, 21 March 1997, p. 17.

91. Radio program, 3 December 1996, text available on the DSS's official website at URL: http://www.dss.org.yu/arhiva/intervju96.html

92. Interview with Vojislav Koštunica by Radmila Stanković, 'Između Đinđića i mene nikad nije bilo nijedne reći o ujedinjenju DS i DSS' [There was never a single word between Đinđić and me about uniting the DS and DSS], *Telegraf International* (Belgrade), 12 December 1995, p. 9.

93. Radio program, 4 December 1996, text available online on the DSS's official website at URL: http://www.dss.org.yu/arhiva/intervju96.html

94. Vojislav Koštunica, 'Serbs and the West: the road ahead,' 10 October 2000 [apparently a reprint of an article first written in January 2000], Rockford Institute website at URL: http://www.rockfordinstitute.org/NewsST101000.htm

95. Interview with Vojislav Koštunica by Igor Jovanović, 'Komadanje Jugoslavije biće nastavljeno' [Yugoslavia's cutting up into pieces will continue], *Bre!* (Belgrade), no. 5, no date supplied, but before the September 2000 elections, online at URL: www.bre.co.yu/arhiva/brojevi/broj5/vojislavKoštunica.htm

96. *NIN*, 2 December 1994, p. 17.

97. *Duga*, 13–19 May 1995, p. 20.

98. *Duga*, 13–19 May 1995, p. 19.

99. *Duga*, 13–19 May 1995, p. 22.

100. *Duga*, 13–19 May 1995, p. 20.

101. *Duga*, 13–19 May 1995, p. 19.

102. *NIN*, 21 March 1997, p. 15.

103. Radio program, 10 December 1996, text available on the DSS's official website at
    URL: http://www.dss.org.yu/arhiva/intervju96.html

104. Radio program, 10 December 1996, text available on the DSS's official website at
    URL: http://www.dss.org.yu/arhiva/intervju96.html
    Jovan Dučić was a extreme nationalist poet and diplomat who died in the U.S. in 1943, and whose reburial in Bosnia-Herzegovina in October 2000 was the occasion for a religious-nationalist event (see below).

105. *Duga*, 13–19 May 1995, p. 20.

106. *NIN*, 28 July 1995, p. 21.

107. *Telegraf International*, 12 December 1995, p. 8.

108. *Javnost*, 26 October 1996, p. 15.

109. *Javnost*, 26 October 1996, p. 15.

110. Vojislav Koštunica quoted in 'Uludo trošenje energije' [Useless waste of energy], *NIN*, 2 July 1998, p. 17.

111. *Duga*, 12–25 September 1998, p. 8.

112. *Duga*, 12–25 September 1998, p. 9.

113. *Duga*, 12–25 September 1998, p. 10.

114. *Duga*, 12–25 September 1998, p. 10

115. Koštunica explained the photo somewhat lamely by claiming that: 'That was a symbolic gesture of support to those who have been abandoned by all' and elsewhere that: 'I would have insulted the locals if I had refused to take the weapon in my hands.' Respectively, *Duga*, 12–25 September 1998, p. 11, and *NIN*, 10 August 2000, p. 15. Indeed, according to Skender Hoti, President of Kosovo's Republican Party, Koštunica on 29 December 1999 reportedly came to Serb-controlled northern Mitrovica and spoke at a rally, whipping up a crowd of local Serbs, who then attacked and ransacked the Republican Party's offices and threw grenades at houses still inhabited by non-Serbs, while Koštunica pressed the local French peacekeepers to prevent Hoti from reopening his office in northern Mitrovica. Personal information by Mr Hoti to the author, Mitrovica, May 2001. At the very least, this would suggest the potential for a cavalier and reckless attitude on the part of Koštunica toward the use of violence in conflict situations.

116. *Duga*, 12–25 September 1998, p. 10.

117. On this period, see Noel Malcolm, *Kosovo; A Short History* (London: Macmillan, 1998), pp. 264–88; Branko Horvat, *Kosovsko pitanje* [*The Kosovo Issue*] (Zagreb: Globus, 1988); and Tomislav Sekulić, *Seobe kao sudbina* [*Exodus as Fate*] (Prishtina: Novi svet, 1994), pp. 48–59.

118. *NIN*, 25 February 1999, p. 21.

119. *NIN*, 25 February 1999, p. 21.

120. *Duga*, 11–24 September 1999, p. 10.

121. *Bre!*, no. 5, 2000.

122. Quoted in 'Putin i Koštunica: Za poštovanje Rezolucije 1244 SB' [Putin and Koštunica: in favor of respecting Security Council Resolution 1244], Radio B-92 (Belgrade), online at URL: http://www.b92.net/archive/s/index.phtml?Y=2001&M=06&D=17

and 'Opasno je bilo kakvo menjanje granica na Balkanu' [Any change in the borders in the Balkans would be dangerous], *Glas javnosti*, 18 June 2001, online at URL: http://www.glas-javnosti.co.yu/arhiva/2001/06/18/srpski/P01061703.shtml

and P. Pašić, 'Rusija za doslednu primenu Rezolucije 1244 o Kosmetu' [Russia favors a consistent implementation of Resolution 1244 on Kosovo], *Glas javnosti*, 18 June 2001, online at URL: http://www.glas-javnosti.co.yu/arhiva/2001/06/18/srpski/P01061701.shtml

123. *Vreme*, 20 September 2000.

124. *NIN*, 21 March 1997, p. 16.

125. *Duga*, 12–25 September 1998, p. 11.

126. Momčilo Pantelić, 'Put obnove duha' [Path to renewing the soul], *Pravoslavlje* (Belgrade), 15 December 2000, p. 1.

127. Ćosić quoted in 'Koštunica i opozicija garantuju promene' [Koštunica and the opposition guarantee changes], *Blic* (Belgrade), 11 September 2000, online at

URL: http://blic.gates96.com

In addition, Koštunica is a native of Serbia, unlike his principal rival Đindić. In an interview granted shortly before his arrest, Slobodan Milošević also expressed his sympathy for Koštunica: 'Koštunica is better than the others [in DOS]; it seems that he wants to defend national interests, but he is weak.' Interview from late March 2001 with Slobodan Milošević by Fulvio Grimaldi, reporter for the Communist daily *Liberazione* (Rome), which apparently declined to publish the article. Available online at URL: http://www.ecn.org/lists/internazionale/200104/msg00013.html

128. Kuhn, pp. 64, 92. Political leaders, of course, can and do change their paradigms, whether out of conviction or political interest, as was the case of Montenegro's President, Milo Đukanović, who had started out as a hardline Serb nationalist but who later became a moderate on inter-ethnic issues.

129. Jervis, p. 412. Howard Margolis reinforces this view: 'In principle, even deeply entrenched habits [i.e. paradigms] can always be challenged if there is evidence and argument that yields intuitions that conflict with those prompted by the habit. In practice, that does not happen easily, sometimes

even when evidence and argument that in hindsight look compelling are available. In some ways changing a habit of mind will be more difficult than changing a physical habit.' *Paradigms & Barriers; How Habits of Mind Govern Scientific Beliefs* (Chicago: Chicago University Press, 1973), pp. 16–17.

130. 'Evidence is being ignored, misremembered, or twisted to preserve old ideas . . .' and 'Because established theories give a coherent, interrelated view of reality, contradicting facts cannot be appreciated until a theory is displaced.' Jervis, pp. 154 and 169.

131. *Telegraf International*, 12 December 1995, p. 8.

132. *Argument*, 14 August 1995, p. 14.

133. Interview with Vojislav Koštunica by RAI, the Italian national radio, 'Serbia: il vento democratico di Koštunica' [Serbia: Koštunica's democratic wind], 12 October 2000, online at
URL: http://www.ilfatto.rai.it/20001012IN.htm

134. Interview with Vojislav Koštunica by Safeta Biševac, 'Miloševićeva odgovornost veća je od jednog stambenog slučaja' [Milošević's responsibility is greater than just a case over an apartment], *Danas* (Belgrade), 3–4 March 2001, online at
URL: http://www.danasnews.com/20010303/tema.html
In fact, it was Koštunica who was most opposed to granting amnesty to Albanian rebels in Preševo when a deal was struck in May 2001, labeling as 'disturbing' the fact that all rebels who laid down their arms would be amnestied, since that would include those 'who committed crimes.' J. Lukač, 'Kosovsko pitanje ostaje otvoreno' [The Kosovo question remains open], *Danas*, 24 May 2001, online at
URL: http://www.danasnews.com/20010524/hronika2.htm

135. Interview with Vojislav Koštunica on RTV Srbija, reported in 'Ne smemo dozvoliti provokaciju poput Račka' [We cannot allow a provocation like Račak], *Politika* (Belgrade), 27 December 2000, online at
URL: http://www.politika.co.yu/2000/1127/01_06a.htm

136. *Danas*, 3–4 March 2001.

137. Vojislav Koštunica, 'Znamo sta hoćemo' [We know what we want], *Vojska* (Belgrade), 11 January 2001, p. 4.

138. As Sandole has noted, Realpolitik entails a perspective by decision-makers according to which they must do everything to defend basic interests such as the survival of the group and of the elite's role, while the 'only morality is successful defense of those interests.' While flexible in some ways, according to Sandole, this nevertheless is a power-based, adversarial, confrontational, zero-sum approach, and one often leading to destructive outcomes: 'Paradigms, theories, and metaphors in conflict and conflict resolution,' p. 4.

139. *Glas javnosti*, 8 December 2001.

140. John Burton, *Resolving Deep-Rooted Conflicts: A Handbook* (Lanham, Maryland: University Press of America, 1987), p. 17.

141. *Danas*, 3–4 March 2001.

142. *Duga*, 11–24 September 1999, p. 9.

143. According to Miloš Radulović, a vice-President of Koštunica's DSS, goals can be achieved more effectively using methods different from those which Milošević had employed. Speaking of the return of Yugoslav forces to the security zones bordering on Kosovo, for example, he assessed that 'The return of our forces to the entire territory of the security zone proves that such a goal can be achieved by means of a wise, principled, and patient policy, without confrontation and without stands which, until the fall of the previous regime, were present within the ruling circles.' DSS press conference of 5 June 2001, on the DSS's website, online at
    URL: http://www.dss.org.yu/prikazi.asp?broj=1709

144. 'It is only aggression that calls forth defense, and war along with it. The aggressor is always peace-loving . . . he would prefer to take over our country unopposed.' Carl von Clausewitz, *On War*, ed. and trans. Michael Howard and Peter Paret (Princeton: Princeton University Press, 1984), p. 370.

145. Interview with Vojislav Koštunica in the Vienna weekly *Profil*, as reported in 'Rešenje u minimalnoj i funkcionalnoj federaciji' [The solution is in a minimal and functional federation], *Blic*, 3 May 2001, online at
    URL: http://blic.gate96.com/danas/broj/strane/politika.htm

146. Slobodan Reljić, 'Koštunica i uvela nadanja' [Koštunica and the faded hopes], *NIN*, 19 October 2000, p. 46–8.

147. Interview with Vojislav Koštunica on the Serb Orthodox Church's official Radio Svetigora, Cetinje, 17 October 2000, online at URL: http://www.mitropolija.cg.yu/aktuelno/intervjui/intervju_Koštunica.html
    In late July 2001, Koštunica signed a 'Protocol of Cooperation' with the SDS on behalf of the DSS. In an accompanying news conference, he characterized the agreement as 'the formalization of a cooperation extending over many years' and stressed that both parties shared the linking of 'the national with the democratic'. S. Ristić, 'Dokument o prijateljstvu' [Document on friendship], *Politika*, 31 July 2001, online edition at
    URL:http://www.politika.co.yu/2001/0731/01_19a.htm
    At the very least, the symbolic impact of reasserting the DSS's shared values and outlook with the hardline SDS is significant.

148. Typically, Mladen Ivanić, Republika Srpska's premier, was buoyed by the agreement, since he saw it as enshrining the right for 'two parts of the same nation to cooperate closely,' and he was confident when he concluded that with respect to the agreement 'there will be plenty of meat in the *burek* [pie],' interview by Orijana Đuđić, 'Veza sa SRJ nije burek bez mesa' [The link with the FRY is not a pie without meat], *Blic*, 7 May 2001, online at

URL: http://blic.gates96.com/danas/broj/strane/intervju.htm

149. Zoran Radisavljević, 'Večni mir pesnika u Hercegovačkoj Gračanici' [Eternal peace for the poet in Gračanica in Herzegovina], *Politika*, 23 October 2000, online at
URL: http://www.politika.co.yu/2000/1023/k01.htm
and Petar Pašić, 'Dučić i sloboda su došli zajedno' [Dučić and freedom came together], Trebinje municipality homepage, 23 October 2000, online at
URL: http://www.trebinje.com/cgi-bin/printthis.cgi?page=558

150. Significantly, Koštunica appears to share some of Dučić's extreme ideas, such as the latter's labeling of all Croats, even those who sat in the Yugoslav government-in-exile during World War II, as genocidal. See Koštunica's favorable quoting of Dučić to that effect in *Duga*, 13–19 May 1995, p. 19.

151. Interview with Predrag Simić by Ljiljana Milić, 'Milošević je bio lak na okidaču' [Milošević was quick on the trigger], *Republika* (Banja Luka), 8 March 2001, online at
URL: http://www.republika-glas.com/62-14.html

152. *Danas*, 3–4 March 2001.

153. One of the DSS's vice-presidents noted that: 'At one time we also seriously considered the concept of regionalism . . . exactly like the Spanish model,' suggesting that this was no longer the case. Interview with Goran Bulajić by Milić Miljenović, 'Mene je Koštunica izabrao' [Koštunica selected me], *Dnevnik* (Novi Sad), 3 June 2001, online at
URL: http://www.dnevnik.co.yu/Strane/intervju.htm

154. As he has stressed, 'Every change in borders in the region will revive smoldering ambitions for new statelets and there we are, perhaps, again in the maelstrom of new conflicts, perhaps even armed ones, in the maelstrom of crises and instability.' Interview with Vojislav Koštunica by Srđan Radulović, 'Srbija neće s nezavisnom Crnom Gorom u savez' [Serbia will not be in a union with an independent Montenegro], *Blic*, 19 April 2001, online at
URL: http://blic.gates96.com/danas/broj/strane/politika.htm

155. As reported by Medija Klub, 7 August 2000, online at URL: www.medijaklub.co.yu/arhiva1/yu/Vijesti/dnevne-vijesti7-8.htm

156. *Danas*, 3–4 March 2001. Reports later emerged that the Yugoslav federal government may have financed the pro-Yugoslav parties in Montenegro during the campaign by means of some covert funding through the federal administration. See J.S., 'Bura u SNP-u povodom optužbi srpskog ministra poljoprivrede' [Storm in the SNP on the heels of the Serbian agriculture minister's accusation], *Vijesti* (Podgorica), 7 May 2001, online at URL: http://www.vijesti.cg.yu/arhiva.phtml?akcija=vijest&id=30407

157. *Danas*, 3–4 March 2001.

158. Quoted in Dubravka Vujanović, 'Žašto Srbiji treba Jugoslavija?' [Why

does Serbia need Yugoslavia?], *Nedeljni telegraf* (Belgrade), 2 May 2001, p. 7.

159. *Danas*, 3–4 March 2001.

160. Interview with Vojislav Koštunica by Nenad Zafirović, Serbian Service, Voice of America, 5 January 2001, online at
URL: http://www.voa.gov/serbian/JAN/Koštunica5jan.html

161. Pro-FRY Montenegrin leader Predrag Bulatović quoted in 'Saradnja bez izručenja' [Cooperation without extradition], *Večernje novosti* (Belgrade), 13 May 2001, online at URL: http://www.novosti.co.yu/default.asp? Kategorija = 1&PDatum = 5/13/2001

162. Koštunica quoted in Duško Vukajlović, 'Buš se založio za celovitu Jugoslaviju' [Bush committed himself to a united Yugoslavia], *Blic*, 10 May 2001, online at
URL: http://blic.gates96.com/danas/broj/strane/politika.htm

163. 'Milošević conscience "clear" over Balkans.' CNN, 13 December 2000, online at URL: http://www.cnn.com/2000/WORLD/europe/12/12/ belgrade/milosevic/index.html

164. *Glas javnosti*, 8 December 2000. Also see his press conference of 13 February 2001, where he said that 'The moment will come when the international community no longer will be able to say that now is not the time for the Yugoslav Army to return to Kosmet,' reported in M. Pešić, 'Nema pregovora sa teroristima' [There will be no negotiations with terrorists], *Politika*, 14 February 2001, online at
URL: http://www.politika.co.yu/2001/0214/01_02.htm

165. *Danas*, 3–4 March 2001. Koštunica continued to promote the return of Belgrade's Army to Kosovo, as in a press conference on 26 June 2001, when he claimed that 'Resolution 1244 allows for a set number of our forces to enter the territory of Kosovo within a set timeline,' and estimated that their return by spring 2002 was 'completely realistic.' 'Nema izručenje pre donatorske konferencije' [There will be no extradition prior to the donors' conference], *Politika*, 27 June 2001, online at
URL: http://www.politika.co.yu/2001/0627/01_01.htm
Even if Koštunica did not believe such completely unrealistic projections, his repeated statements to that effect would have a clearly inflammatory impact and set back prospects for conflict resolution on Kosovo.

166. Interview with General Nebojša Pavković by Petar Pašić, 'Spremni smo i za Kosmet!' [We are also ready for Kosmet!], *Glas javnosti*, 26 May 2001, online at URL: http://arhiva.glas-javnosti.co.yu/arhiva/2001/05/26/ srpski/P01052501.shtml
Again, in June 2001, Lt-Col. General Ninoslav Krstić, Commander of the Joint Security Force which took control of the buffer zone, assured Yugoslav audiences that 'The Yugoslav Army has announced its readiness

to use that [Third Task Force] contingent to return to Kosovo and Metohija in a peaceful manner.' Interview with General Krstić by Petar Pašić, 'Vraćamo se i na Kosmet!' [We will also return to Kosmet!] , *Glas javnosti*, 10 June 2001, online at URL: http://www.arhiva.glas-javnosti.co.yu/2001/06/10/srpski/I01060901.shtml

167. Interview with Hans Haekkerup, 'Beograd nam šalje signale da nastavimo rad na pravnom okviru za kosovsku samoupravu' [Belgrade is sending us signals that we should continue our work on a legal framework for Kosovo's self-government], *Danas*, 21–22 April 2001, online at URL: http://www.danasnews.com/20010421/vikend3.htm

168. Quoted in 'Koštunica zatražio ukidanje carinskih punktova' [Koštunica sought the abrogation of the customs points], *Politika*, 19 April 2001, online at URL: http//:www.politika.co.yu/2001/0419/01_09.htm

169. This was DSS Vice-President Marko Jakšić's argument at a press conference, 1 May 2001, DSS website at URL: http://www.dss.org.yu/prikazi.asp?broj=1692

170. See the interview with Goran Bulajić, *Dnevnik*, 3 June 2001.

171. On these relations, see Zvonko Tarle, 'KFOR protect bishop from angry flock,' April 2000, online at Serb Orthodox Church's official website in Kosovo, online at URL: http://www.decani.yunet.com/archive_ apr2.html and Dejan Anastasijević, 'Mostar on the Ibar,' *Vreme*, 28 August 1999, online at URL: http://www.cdsp.neu.edu/info/students/marko/vreme/vreme53.html

172. N. Smikić, 'Kfor nas neće pokolebati' [KFOR will not make us waver], *Glas javnosti*, 21 April 2001, online at URL: http://arhiva.glas-javnosti.co.yu/arhiva/2001/04/21/srpski/P01042006.shtml As in Vojvodina, in Serb-controlled northern Kosovo Koštunica's DSS is reported to be working in a coalition with Šešelj's SRS and with Milošević's SPS, M. Laketić, 'Novi raskoli – stari krivci' [New splits – same ones guilty], *Politika*, 8 June 2001, online at URL: http://www.politika.co.yu/2001/0608/01_05.htm

173. Press conference of 1 May 2001, on the DSS website at URL: http://www.dss.org.yu/prikazi.asp?broj=1692

174. Quoted in 'Nije vreme za ustav' [This is not the time for a constitution], *Glas javnosti*, 11 April 2001, online at URL: http://arhiva.glas-javnosti.co.yu/arhive/2001/04/11/srpski/P01041002.shtml

175. Interview with Rada Trajković by Jelena Tasić, 'Dnevni problemi odvlače vlast od kosovskog pitanja' [Daily problems distract the government from the Kosovo issue], *Danas*, 3 May 2001, online at URL: http://www.danasnews.com/20010503/hronika4.htm

176. For example, asked in 1998 whether he thought the partition of Kosovo

was a good idea, he had replied that 'I do not think that is either a good or a feasible solution.' *Duga*, 12–25 September 1998, p. 9.

177. For example, when asked about his view of partition now, Koštunica dismissed the option: 'Such a proposal should not take up our time, for the simple reason that until such time as the unimpeded return of the Serbs and the other non-Albanian population is secured, by accepting this concept we would be freezing the status quo in Kosovo, which is extremely unfavorable to us.' V. Đorđević, 'Milošević nije uslov' [Milošević is not a precondition], *Glas javnosti*, 24 May 2001, online at URL: http://arhiva.glas-javnosti.co.yu/arhiva/2001/05/24/srpski/P01052302.shtml

178. Interview with Zoran Lutovac by Jelena Jovović, 'Na snazi stare ucene' [Old blackmail still in force], *Večernje novosti*, 2 June 2001, online at URL: http://www.novosti.co.yu

179. Interview with Dragan Lazić by Ljiljana Staletović, 'Nove mape, so na živu ranu' [New maps; salt on open wounds], *Glas javnosti*, 13 June 2001, online at URL: http://www.glas-javnosti.co.yu/danas/srpski/X01061201.shtml

180. In 1991, there were only five municipalities (*opštine*) in Kosovo where Serbs were a majority, but this itself was the result of recent gerrymandering, since in 1981 there had only been one such municipality. As it is, those areas with a Serb majority in 1991 were sparsely settled, and represented only 2.7 per cent of Kosovo's total population. See Bogoljub Kočović, *Etnički i demografski razvoj u Jugoslaviji od 1921. do 1991. godine* [*The Ethnic and Demographic Development of Yugoslavia from 1921 to 1991*] (Paris: Bibliothèque Dialogue, 1998), pp. 496–9.

181. For example, he has spoken of 500,000 refugees from Kosovo, which is patently several-fold above the true figure; interview with Vojislav Koštunica by Amir Tahiri, 'Koštunica li-l-Sharq al-Awsat: La yanbaghi an yudghit al-gharb 'alayna bi-shidda li-taslim al-muhtammin bi-jara'im harb' [The West should not pressure us intensely to hand over those accused of war crimes], *Al-Sharq al-Awsat* (London,)15 February 2001, p. 7. Elsewhere, he has claimed that 300,000 Serbs lived in Kosovo (that, too, is too high), compounding that by asserting that this figure represented a third or quarter of the total population, rather than a more accurate tenth. See 'Intervju – Vojislav Koštunica' [Interview – Vojislav Koštunica], *Nezavisne novine* (Toronto), 24 November 2000, online at URL: http://www.nezavisnenovine.com/ARHIVA/2000/24_11_00/yu.html

182. Reported in M. Petrović, 'Koštunica: SRJ nema više vremena za gubljenje' [Yugoslavia has no more time to lose], *Politika*, 2 June 2001, online at URL: http://www.politika.co.yu/2001/0602/01_07.htm
    Such assessments today are overdrawn. As the author can attest from a visit to Kosovo in May 2001, Serb Orthodox sites were adequately protected, and even the Orthodox cathedral built in the 1990s right on

the campus of the University of Prishtina appeared safe, although it was protected by only one guard.

183. As he put it: 'Israeli-Palestinian relations can be compared to the Serbian-Albanian ones', *Ha'aretz*, 26 November 2000.

184. 'Nationalist indoctrination among the Albanians has reached an incredibe intensity . . . Personally, I believe that it is premature for any negotiations with the Albanians so long as their nationalist mobilization lasts.' Interview with Predrag Simić, *Republika*, 8 March 2001.

185. Interview with Vojislav Koštunica to the Czech daily *Pravo*, reported in 'Izbori nisu mogući bez promene položaja Srba' [Elections are not possible without a change in the situation of the Serbs], *Blic*, 22 May 2001, online at URL: http://blic.gates96.com/arhiva/200105022/strane/politika.htm

186. *Pravo* apud *Blic*, 22 May 2001.

187. CBS correspondent Scott Pelley, however, denied any distortion and reported of Koštunica that: 'He was very evasive, particularly on the Milošević question. We had to go back to him again and again and again to get a straight answer.' According to an Associated Press report by Katarina Kratovac, 'Koštunica says his words on Kosovo were taken out of context by CBS,' online at
URL: http://www.freepublic.com/forum/a39fb0a551353.htm

188. 'Intervju – Vojislav Koštunica' [Interview – Vojislav Koštunica], *Nezavisne novine*, 24 November 2000, online at URL: http://www.nezavisnenovine.com/ARHIVA/2000/24_11_00/yu.html

189. *Nezavisne novine*, 24 November 2000.

190. Interview with Vojislav Koštunica by Milan Mijailović, 'Budućnost je u zajedničkoj državi' [The future is in a joint state], *Glas javnosti*, 14–16 April 2001, online at
URL: http://www.glas-javnosti.co.yu/danas/srpski/I01041301.shtml

191. RAI, 12 October 2000. Koštunica likewise told *Time* magazine that 'when it comes to war crimes, there were war crimes committed by NATO last year.' Interview with Vojislav Koštunica, 'This is more than a velvet revolution,' *Time*, 23 October 2000, online at
URL: http://www.time/europe/magazine/2000/1023/Koštunica.html

192. Quoted in M. Pešić, 'Nema pregovora sa teroristima' [There will be no negotiations with terrorists], *Politika*, 14 February 2001, online at
URL: http://www.politika.co.yu/2001/0214/01_02.htm

193. Interview with Koštunica in the diaspora newspaper *Vesti* (Frankfurt), reported as 'Dijaspori dati pravo glasa' [Give the right to vote to the diaspora], *Glas javnosti*, 7 February 2001, online at URL: http://arhiva.glas-javnosti.co.yu/arhiva/2001/02/07/srpski/P01020613.shtml

Koštunica has retained his focus on blaming NATO for war crimes and has used this as a means not only to diminish the Tribunal's legitimacy but to divert calls for a genuine self-examination of the recent past within

Serbia. As he maintained, 'In discussions about The Hague today, a so-called moral catharsis is often brought up. I do not know what moral catharsis is. There have been no end of crimes in wars throughout history and no one has ever thought of talking about a catharsis. There is no moral catharsis without a catharsis which senior NATO officials, who are responsible for bombing this country in 1999, would also go through. That would be a moral catharsis.' Interview with Vojislav Koštunica, 'Mučna saradnja' [Painful cooperation], *Vreme*, 5 July 2001, online at URL: http://www.vreme.com/cms/view.php?id=291433

194. *Danas*, 3–4 March 2001.

195. *Vesti* apud *Glas javnosti*, 7 February 2001.

196. See Koštunica's argument in *Danas*, 3–4 March, 2001.

197. Koštunica speaking at a Holocaust commemoration, 'Sećanje za žrtve holokausta' [Remembering the victims of the Holocaust], *Politika*, 19 April 2001, online at
   URL: http://www.politika.co.yu/2001/0419/01_07a.htm
   According to Vladan Batić, Serbia's Minister of Justice, the strategy of apportioning equal blame to all ('All are responsible, that is my answer') also has a practical motivation. As Batić argued, if only the Serb leadership is indicted, that would mean that Serbia fought wars of aggression, which would make it automatically liable to pay compensation, while Serbia would then not be able eventually to sue for compensation for damage caused by NATO. Interview with Vladan Batić, 'Sada je potrebno hleba i pravde' [Now bread and justice are needed], *Glas javnosti*, 26–27 April 2001, online at
   URL: http//www.glas-javnosti.co.yu/danas/srpski/I01042502.shtml

198. *Al-Sharq al-Awsat*, 15 February 2001, p. 7.

199. Interview with Vojislav Koštunica by Aleksandr Liubimov. 'Voislav Koshtunitsa nalazhivaet kontakty' [Vojislav Koštunica repairs contacts], ORT Television (Moscow), 26 October 2000, online at
   URL: http://alyona.nns.ru/interv/int2476.html
   In a press conference, Koštunica assessed that compensation for NATO damages would run to Ð30 billion, 'Najviše odgovoran svom narodu' [Responsible most to one's own nation], *Dnevnik*, 4 April 2001, online at
   URL: http://www.dnevnik.co.yu/Strane/aktuelna.htm
   In Koštunica's view, his stand on the Tribunal continues to be valid: 'First of all, in the assessment that the truth which this court expresses is selective, that the Hague Tribunal is biased, and that this court is not very much of a court. It is not international, even though it is called that. It is for all intents and purposes a court of specific powerful countries and specific interests, more American than international. Even before Slobodan Milošević's departure for The Hague that cooperation was painful to me, and after all that has happened it is even more painful.' *Vreme*, 5 July 2001. He further complained that the Tribunal 'showed proved bias in

selecting those who have been tried up to now. I will repeat, most of those are from the Federal Republic of Yugoslavia and from Republika Srpska, most are from the political and military leadership, the very top of the Yugoslav and Serb political and military elite.' Interview with Vojislav Koštunica by Jovo Vukelić, 'Koštunica: Rasplet zahteva nove izbore u SRJ i Srbiji' [Koštunica: discussion on the request for new elections in Yugoslavia and Serbia], *Politika*, 11 July 2001, online at

URL: http://www.politika.co.yu/2001/0711/01_01.htm

Despite Milošević's unavoidable extradition, Koštunica may well seek to derail further cooperation with the Tribunal.

200. *Glas javnosti*, 14–16 April 2001.

201. Interview with Vojislav Koštunica by Nathan Gardels, 'Koštunica: 'Adalat mahkamat La Hay 'adala intiqamiyya' [Koštunica: the justice of the Hague Tribunal is the justice of revenge], *al-Sharq al-Awsat*, 2 February 2001, p. 7.

202. Mensur Čamo, 'Novi zahtijev SRJ Medjunarodnom sudu pravde u den Haagu – Nova kupovina vremena' [The SRJ's new request to the International Court of Law in the Hague – a new attempt to buy time], Radio Free Europe, 27 April 2001, online at

URL: http://www.danas.org/programi/haaska

203. Interview with Vojislav Koštunica by Beatrice Ottaviano, 'Koštunica: "Ballottaggio illegale. Milošević e finito"' [Koštunica: 'Illegal election. Milošević is finished'], *Il Giorno* (Milan), 3 October 2000, online at

URL: http://ilgiorno.monrif.net

204. Quoted in Steven Erlanger, 'Yugoslav firm on his stand to bar Milošević from Hague,' *New York Times*, 2 April 2001, online at URL: http://www.nytimes.com

205. *Danas*, 3–4 March 2001.

206. *Danas*, 3–4 March 2001.

207. Interview with Carla Del Ponte, 'Il procuratore Carla Del Ponte: "Lo scontro tra l'Aja e Belgrado"' [Prosecutor Carla Del Ponte: 'The clash between The Hague and Belgrade'], CNN Italia, 27 January 2001, online at URL: www.cnnitalia.it/2001/MONDO/europa/01/26/delponte

208. *Danas*, 3–4 March 2001.

209. *Danas*, 3–4 March 2001.

210. Quoted in S[afeta] Biševac, 'Vojska je radila po zakonu' [The army acted according to the law], *Danas*, 4 April 2001, online at URL: www.danasnews.com/20010404/hronika2.htm

211. 'We will have an entire field of cooperation with The Hague when it is the case of documentation; here we have hit on something which is very important and where The Hague has not adequately cooperated up to now. When I say this, I am thinking about the documentation which was

delivered to The Hague and which in some cases was lost, as was the case with [Croatian war crimes in] Gospić and with the Albanian crimes in Kosovo . . . There were also criticisms in 1999 on the contravention of the norms of international humanitarian law during the [NATO] airstrikes, which also was avoided.' *Glas javnosti*, 14–16 April 2001.

212. Press conference by President Koštunica, 3 April 2001, reported in 'Svet više duguje nama nego mi njemu' [The world owes us more than we owe it], *Politika*, 4 April 2001, online at
URL: http://www.politika.co.yu/2001/0404/01_01.htm

213. Interview with Dragan Mašrićanin by Dubravka Vujanović, 'Novi izbori su potreba i neminovnost!' [New elections are needed and are inevitable], *Nedeljni telegraf*, 6 June 2001, online at
URL: http://www.nedeljnitelegraf.co.yu/novi/marsh.html

214. For Mašrićanin, the international community's insistence on Milošević's extradition in exchange for economic aid was in itself beyond the pale: 'Without a doubt, this is a question of the renewal of the old practice of blackmailing the Yugoslav government.' *Nedeljni telegraf*, 6 June 2001.

215. Quoted in 'Vojska je radila po zakonu' [The army acted according to the law], *Danas*, 4 April 2001, online at
URL: http://www.danasnews.com/200010404/hronika2.htm

216. Koštunica, for example, had promised a visiting delegation from Milošević's party that no extradition would occur before a lengthy judicial review of the extradition decree, according to Zoran Anđelković, a senior SPS official: Lj. Begenišić, 'Nema izručivanje pre odluke Ustavnoga suda' [There will not be any extradition prior to the Constitutional Court's decision], *Blic*, 28 June 2001, online at
URL: http://blic.gates96.com/danas/broj/strane/politika.htm
Indeed, Koštunica's strategy apparently had been to begin legal procedures against Milošević at home in order to postpone his extradition, 'and then, since nothing is immutable and everything changes, even the Tribunal, [we could] gain some time', *Vreme*, 5 July 2001.

217. Koštunica rued that the extradition had occurred only because he and his party were a minority in the coalition government Aleksandar Vasović, 'Milošević extradition result of US push,' *Washington Times*, 27 June 2001, p. A15. He also called the extradition 'demeaning' and insisted that it could 'not be viewed as legal and constitutional.' Quoted in D.G. and V.P., 'Ishitreno i ponižavajuće' [Overhasty and demeaning], *Glas javnosti*, 29 June 2001, online at URL: http://arhiva.glas-javnosti.co.yu/arhiva/2001/06/29/srpski/P01062838.shtml

218. On claims by other government officials tthat Koštunica did know, see 'I Koštunica bio za izručenje' [Koštunica too was in favor of extradition], *Glas javnosti*, 30 June 2001, online at URL: http://arhiva.glas-javnosti.co.yu/arhiva/2001/06/30/srpski/P01062905.shtml
On Koštunica's counterclaim that he did not know and still disagreed

with the decision, see 'Nisam bio obaveŝten' [I was not informed], *Glas javnosti*, 1 July 2001, online at URL: http://arhiva.glas-javnosti.co.yu/arhiva/2001/07/01/srpski/P01063010.shtml

Significantly, Koŝtunica continued to describe the extradition as 'illegal, unconstitutional, and irresponsible' and called the act 'an attempt at a limited coup d'état'. Interview with Vojislav Koŝtunica, 'Koŝtunica: Mi sento come un ostaggio' [I feel like a hostage], *La Stampa*,(Turin), 8 July 2001, online at
URL: http://www.lastampa.it

DSS spokesmen were quick to underline that the differences within the coalition went far beyond the extradition. According to the president of the DSS's new parliamentary caucus, Dejan Mihajlov, the DSS, 'after a series of decisions with which we could not agree , decided to establish its own parliamentary caucus.' Interview with Dejan Mihajlov by Sredoje Simić, 'Možda je zalogaj koji je vlada krenula da zagrize prevelik, pa se zagrcnula!" [Perhaps the government bit off more than it could chew!], *Svedok*, July 2001, no. 260, online at
URL: http://www.svedok.co.yu/index.asp?show=26003

Koŝtunica went on to complain that, as a result of being bypassed on the extradition, 'I really feel like a hostage at several levels', blaming not only former Milošević supporters but also his fellow coalition partners and 'merciless international pressure which is completely without justification', *La Stampa*, 8 July 2001.

219. Koŝtunica's claim that it would be 'complicated' for the Commission to call witnesses, and his decision not to have a link with the courts since 'no court could offer the whole truth', is suggestive of the body's likely role. His conclusion that the Commission's primary mission was 'for us to confront the truth and to reconcile ourselves with each other' suggested primarily a Serb-Serb focus. *Blic*, 19 April 2001.

220. Vojislav Koŝtunica, 'Žal za Miloševićem' [Regretting Milošević], *NIN*, 8 March 2001, online at
URL: http://www.nin.co.yu/2001-0308/16954.html

221. With Milošević's ouster, for example, Koŝtunica believed that Belgrade's future prospects in Kosovo would improve, since there would no longer be in Belgrade an individual not recognized by the international community. *NIN*, 10 August 2000, p. 15.

222. *Vreme*, 20 September 2000.

223. Unlike Montenegro, Vojvodina is economically significant, being an agricultural breadbasket and industrial area; it was joined to Serbia in 1945 as an autonomous province, but by 1974 enjoyed the status of a republic for all intents and purposes.

224. Interview with Nenad Čanak in *Republika*, reproduced in 'Koŝtunica velikosrbin, Đinđić ne razume' [Koŝtunica a Great Serbian; Đinđić does not understand], *Dnevnik*, 29 April 2001, online at
URL: http://www.dnevnik.co.yu/Strane/aktuelna/htm

225. See the interview with the latter's vice president, Boris Tadić, 'Autonomija Vojvodine je deo programa DS' [Vojvodina's autonomy is part of the Democratic Party's platform], *Svedok* (Belgrade), No. 245, March 2001, online at
URL: http://www.svedok.co.yu/index.asp?show=97

226. 'Pitanje Vojvodine u okviru DOS-a' [The issue of Vojvodina within the DOS framework], Radio 021 (Novi Sad), 11 April 2001, online at
URL: http://www.vojvodina.com/politika/default.htm

227. Dnevnik, 3 June 2001. Typically, a member of the DSS Council in Vojvodina, Rade Marinkov, blasted requests for greater autonomy as 'leading to separatism': 'Put koji vodi u separatizam' [A path which leads to separatism], *Glas javnosti*, 22 June 2001, online at URL: http://arhiva.glas-javnosti.co.yu/arhiva/2001/06/22/srpski/P01062107.shtml

228. Dennis J. D. Sandole, *Conflict Resolution in the Post-Cold War Era*, ICAR Working Paper No. 6 (Fairfax, Virginia: George Mason University, October 1992), p. 15.

229. RAI, 12 October 2000.

230. Quoted in 'Voislav Koshtunitsa: My dukhovno blizki' [Vojislav Koštunica: We are spiritually close], 28 October 2000, *Trud* (Moscow), online at URL: http://www.trud.ru

231. *Danas*, 3–4 March 2001.

232. *Danas*, 3–4 March 2001.

233. See his views as told to Tim Judah in an interview, 'Goodbye to Yugoslavia?,' *The New York Review of Books*, 8 February 2001, p. 44.

234. *Glas javnosti*, 14–16 April 2001.

235. Reported in 'DSS mora da bude spremna za izbore' [The DSS must be prepared for elections], *Glas javnosti*, 26 March 2001, online at URL: http://www.arhiva.glas-javnosti.co.yu/arhiva/2001/03/226/srpski/P01032502.shtml

236. Interview with Vojislav Koštunica by Nenad Ristić on Serbian State Television, 5 May 2001.

237. Interview with Vojislav Koštunica on the Serb Orthodox Church's official Radio Svetigora (Cetinje), 17 October 2000, online at URL: http://www.mitropolija.cg.yu/aktuelno/intervjui/intervju_Koštunica.html

238. See the DSS party platform, online at
URL: http://www.dss.org.yu/prikazi.asp?rubrika=16

239. *Ha'aretz*, 26 November 2000. It should be noted that the decisive pressure for Milošević's extradition, especially in the form of conditions for international economic aid, depended largely on US efforts, without which the international community might well have caved in long ago to Koštunica's preferred solution. For example, in April 2001, the European Union, lacking a consensus, apparently had concluded that the mere arrest

of Milošević had met its condition for cooperation with the Tribunal; or
at least this was so interpreted in Belgrade, although the Tribunal itself
continued to press for extradition. See 'Izručenje Miloševića nije uslov za
pomoć EU' [Handing over of Milošević is not a condition for EU aid],
Glas javnosti, 10 April 2001, online at URL: http://www.glas-
javnosti.co.yu/danas/srpski/P01040905.shtml

As late as June 2001, the European Commission seemed ambivalent
on linking aid to the extradition, with the latter's spokesman for foreign
affairs noting that 'Milošević's extradition is not a specific condition':
Miša Vidić, 'Izručenje Miloševića nije uslov za donatorsku konferenciju'
[Milošević's extradition is not a condition for the donors' conference],
Politika, 23 June 2001, online at
   URL: http://www.politika.co.yu/2001/0623/01_07.htm

240. RAI, 12 October 2000.

241. RAI, 12 October 2000.

242. Koštunica speaking at the DSS Central Council, *Glas javnosti*, 26 March
2001.

243. Interview with Vojislav Koštunica on BK TV (Belgrade), reported in
'Koštunica: Verujem u opstanak Jugoslavije' [Koštunica: I believe in
Yugoslavia's survival], *Politika*, 9 April 2001, online at
   URL: www.politika.co.yu/2001/0409/01_01.htm

244. See, for example, DSS Vice-President Dragan Mašrićanin's statement that
'elections are not called without there being a great need, and the need
already exists.' Interview with Dragan Mašrićanin by Dubravka Vujanović,
'Novi izbori su potreba i neminovnost!' [New elections are needed and
are inevitable], *Nedeljni telegraf*, 6 June 2001, online at
   URL: http://www.nedeljnitelegraf.co.yu/novi/marsh.html

Mašrićanin also confirmed that 'The limited life of the DOS as a
coalition has been known since it was founded,' and boasted that 'After
all, the DSS today is strong enough to go into the elections on its own and
win the strongest position in the Parliament.' Interview with Dragan
Mašrićanin by Olivera Milivojević, 'DSS je dovoljno jaka da na sledećim
izborima sama obezbedi najuticajnije mesto u parlamentu' [The DSS is
strong enough to win the strongest position in the parliament on its own
in the next elections], *Svedok* , 29 May 2001, online at
   URL: http://www.svedok.co.yu/index.asp?show=25309

245. See the report by Ivo Pukanić and Berislav Jelinić, '*Nacional* razotkriva
kako je djelovala najveća balkanska mafijaška organizacija' [*Nacional*
reveals how the largest Balkan Mafia organization operated], *Nacional*
(Zagreb), 31 May 2001, online at
   URL: http://www.nacional.hr/htm/289007.hr.htm

Information about cadavers of Albanian civilians killed during the
Kosovo War and transported in refrigerated trucks to Serbia for disposal,
which was leaked to the press at about this time, apparently by Dušan

Mihajlović, Serbia's Minister of the Interior, were presumably intended to parry Koštunica's opposition to extradition.

246. Interview with Miodrag Đuričić by Konstantin Kachalin, 'Seryi kardinal Voislava Koshtunitsy' [Vojislav Koštunica's éminence grise], *Vek* (Moscow), 20 October 2000, online at
URL: http://www.wek.ru

247. For example, the DSS set up its own party caucus within Serbia's Parliament, and criticized Serbia's Minister of the Interior (Dušan Mihajlović) and Minister of Justice (Vladan Batić) who had been active in the extradition, suggesting that the two ministries should now be headed by DSS members instead; see 'Izjava Đinđića je zastrašujuća' [Đinđić's statement is frightening], *Glas javnosti*, 4 July 2001, online at
URL: http://www.glas-javnosti.co.yu/danas/srpski/P01070301.shtml
and V. Đorđević, 'Ministarstva pravde i policije za DSS' [The ministries of justice and police for the DSS], *Glas javnosti*, 1 July 2001, online at
URL: http://www.glas-javnosti.co.yu/danas/srpski/P01063018.shtml
DSS spokesmen were quick to underline that the differences within the coalition went far beyond the extradition.

248. The Serbian media have reported that influential leftist political backers have been shifting their allegiance to the DSS in order to protect their positions, which would boost the DSS's resources, although it is unclear how that might influence policy. See 'Pranje biografija, prljanje obraza' [The washing of biographies, the dirtying of honor], *Glas javnosti*, 8 April 2001, online at URL: http://www.glas-javnosti.co.yu/danas/srpski/X)1040701.shtml

249. Interview with Zoran Đinđić in the Warsaw daily *Gazeta Wyborcza*, reported in 'Milošević mora prvo da odgovara u Jugoslaviji' [Milošević must first answer in Yugoslavia], *Blic*, 5 June 2001, online at URL: http://blic.gates96.com/danas/broj/strane/politika.htm
Similarly, despite his differences with Koštunica on many issues, Đinđić, when asked for his view of a division of Kosovo into entities, responded: 'That idea could be assumed to be one of the most realistic solutions: a partition on the model of Bosnia, with Serbs and Albanians living there [i.e. in separate entities].' *El Mundo* , 3 June 2001.

250. *El Mundo*, 3 June 2001.

251. Kuhn, p. 67.

252. I am indebted to Christopher Mitchell of the Institute for Conflict Analysis and Resolution for this insight.

253. Richard E. Rubenstein, *Conflict Resolution and Power Politics; Global Conflict after the Cold War*, ICAR Working Paper (Fairfax, Virginia: George Mason University, January 1996), pp. 1–2.

254. A potential exception was when Koštunica visited the US in May 2001, on which occasion further aid was made conditional on Milošević's

extradition to The Hague: David R. Sands, 'Milošević trial key to aid, US says,' *Washington Times*, 10 May 2001, p. A11.

255. Dennis J. D. Sandole, 'Paradigms, theories, and metaphors in conflict and conflict resolution,' p. 11.

256. 'I wrongly assumed that it would be easier to get rid of various aspects of sanctions, including the American outer wall of sanctions, than to change the image which had been created of our country . . . However, [the picture of our country] changed overnight because those who had demonized us in an instant dropped it very easily. That policy of demonizing the Federal Republic of Yugoslavia, and above all of the Serbs, suffered a defeat.' *Glas javnosti*, 8 December 2000.

257. Koštunica termed his talks in the United States as 'encouraging due to the complete understanding of the American interlocutors for the situation in Yugoslavia, whether on the most sensitive issues such as Kosovo or southern Serbia, or the less sensitive ones such as relations with Montenegro.' Quoted in Duško B. Vukajlović, 'Buš se založio za celovitu Jugoslaviju' [Bush committed himself to a united Yugoslavia], *Blic*, 10 May 2001, online at
URL: http://blic.gates96.com/danas/broj/strane/politika.htm

258. As Koštunica's foreign policy adviser, Predrag Simić, concluded, 'Perhaps some may think that Yugoslavia and its president are just symbols, but it is sufficient to say that American President George Bush does not think so . . . Also, the fact that in New York President Koštunica was presented with the award of Statesman of the Year [by the East West Institute] in and of itself says how much Yugoslavia is a reality as far as the most influential portion of the world is concerned.' Quoted in Dubravka Vujanović, 'Zašto Srbiji treba Jugoslavija?' [Why Serbia needs Yugoslavia], *Nedeljni telegraf*, 2 May 2001, p. 6.

259. David Owen, 'To secure Balkan peace, redraw the map,' *Wall Street Journal*, 13 March 2001, p. A26.

Index

Note: entries for Vojislav Koštunica, Serbia and Serbs are not included.